DAYBREAK

Hazelden Titles of Related Interest

Each Day a New Beginning: Daily Meditations for Women

Worthy of Love: Meditations on Loving Ourselves and Others

The Healing Way: Adult Recovery from Childhood Sexual Abuse, Kristin A. Kunzman

DAYBREAK

Meditations for Women Survivors Of Sexual Abuse

Maureen Brady

A Hazelden Book
HarperCollins*Publishers*

DAYBREAK: *Meditations for Women Survivors of Sexual Abuse.* Copyright © 1991 by Maureen Brady. This edition published by arrangement with the Hazelden Foundation. All rights reserved. Printed in the United States of America. No part of this book may be used or reproduced in any manner whatsoever without written permission except in the case of brief quotations embodied in critical articles and reviews. For information address HarperCollins Publishers, 10 East 53rd Street, New York, NY 10022.

FIRST HARPERCOLLINS EDITION PUBLISHED IN 1991.

Library of Congress Cataloging-in-Publication Data

Brady, Maureen.
    Daybreak : meditations for women survivors
of sexual abuse / Maureen Brady. — 1st
HarperCollins ed.
    p. cm.
    "A Hazelden book."
    ISBN 0–06–255334–8
    1. Adult child sexual abuse victims—Prayer-
books and devotions—English. 2. Women—
Prayer-books and devotions—English. 3. Twelve-
step programs—Religious aspects—Meditations.
    I. Title
BL624.5.B72 1991
362.7'.6—dc20

                       90–56466
                          CIP

91 92 93 94 95 K.P. 10 9 8 7 6 5 4 3 2 1

This edition is printed on acid-free paper which meets the American National Standards Institute Z39.48 Standard

ACKNOWLEDGMENTS

For the inspiration of their journeys I thank the women of my incest survivors' group, for faith in me and the sharing of their wisdom, I thank Pearl Mindell, Stephen Roos, and Helen Turnbull, and for her intelligent editing and her enthusiasm all along the way, I thank my editor, Pat Boland.

INTRODUCTION

Long after the offenses are over and in the past, we who have been violated in childhood by sexual abuse carry with us an internal monologue that goes on discouraging us and tearing us down as we attempt to reconstruct and heal in our recovery. The meditations in this book contain statements that counter this monologue, that encapsulate the ways we would like to think, behave, or feel about ourselves. They point us in the direction we wish to go by helping us create a new vision. Keeping this vision in mind is a tool we can use to intercept our critical, self-deprecatory voices.

Most of us have suffered long years of silence and secrecy about our abuse. We may not even have been aware of it in our memory. Or we may have been painfully plagued by our memories of the abuse but not known how to touch them. Whether we were in touch with our memories or not, most of us had a Pandora's box in which we tried to contain this haunting experience. As we open it and begin to realize the depth to which our life has been affected by the abuse, we begin a healing journey.

Yet because the road we travel is long and full of treacherous curves, we require much encouragement. We find it in one another. We seek daily inspiration and reminders that we are in a process, moving through recovery, not simply subjecting ourselves to further pain. It is my hope that these meditations can serve sexual abuse survivors both as daily inspiration, and also by showing and celebrating our courage. As we bump along this journey, there comes a time when, almost as if by accident, we notice we've begun to thrive.

Many of the meditations refer to incest or the incest survivor.* The effects of childhood sexual abuse by a stranger are similar to those encountered by incest survivors. Thus survivors of sexual abuse by strangers or nonfamily members will, I hope, also find these daily meditations useful to them.

Although I have not addressed sexual abuse recovery issues that are particular to men's experiences, men and women survivors share common ground in their suffering, in many of the effects of the abuse, and certainly in their need for encouragement. I welcome men as well as women to receive the benefits of these meditations.

It may be helpful to read a meditation out loud, whether alone or with someone else, and to then reflect briefly on what it means to you. Keeping in mind the suggestion "identify, don't compare" will allow you to receive greater guidance from these pages.

You have embarked on a courageous journey. May you be blessed and carried along.

---

* I define incest broadly as it is defined in a Twelve Step group modeled after Alcoholics Anonymous, Survivors of Incest Anonymous (SIA), as any sexual behavior imposed on a person by a member of his or her immediate or extended family. "Extended family" might include people you or your family knew over a period of time such as a grandparent, uncle, aunt, in-law, cousin, friend of the family, stepparent, etc. Sexual contacts may include verbal and/or physical behaviors; penetration is not necessary for the definition of incest.

January

The new year lends itself to the hope of new beginnings. I release old resentments and give this year a chance to be a time of renewal.

We must start anew again and again in life. We strive to get ahead of our old injuries, sometimes through escape, sometimes in sincere healing. We might wish that we could move out of our life into someone else's. We might wish that we could complete one healing and never feel those wounds again. But of course this is foolish grappling with the impossible. Real life is lived when we are fully with ourselves, and that means encountering our sources of pain as well as our sources of joy.

I can, however, let go of resentments, make amends where I need to, including to myself, and ask for guidance from my higher power. This will help me release the voices that lead me repeatedly into situations that abuse or deprive me. It may create fear in me not to know where I am going, but that can also be life's adventure. I hold the hand of my inner child as we walk into new ways of living. We keep our eyes and ears open. We allow ourselves pleasure and the hope and excitement of new beginnings.

I am accountable for my behaviors and attitudes and can learn to make repairs when they have hurt others.

In my family of origin, accountability was not modeled. There was a general obliviousness to individual responsibility. I was led to believe that my behavior held the power to shame the entire family, yet I was not shown any simple ways to evaluate and correct my mistakes. Spilled milk did not elicit an "Oops, let's clean it up." Instead the spiller proved to be a bad person and, because of how entangled the family was, the spill held the potential to reflect badly on everyone. This lack of individual accountability enabled the incest perpetrators to mix in and mix up their abuses with everything else.

As I heal I become more aware of the idea that I am always and only responsible for myself. I am relieved to be free of the burden of an entangled family. I learn how I affect others and how to be accountable. If I betray my own values, I can go back and correct my course by making amends and changing what I will do the next time. I can look quietly at myself at the end of each day and finish all business that is bothersome.

I am grateful for laughter and its ability to nourish my soul.

Hearty laughter gives balance to our pain and offers us a sense of well-being. Physiologically, it may even release chemicals into the bloodstream that contribute to relaxation in a way similar to exercise. We all need good regular doses of laughter. Perhaps we who've been abused need it even more than others.

I share with other survivors in my incest group and notice that we often find ways to transform our pain from the darkness of an unbearable event into a laughable description. A woman describes how her father touched her breasts under the auspices of teaching her to drive their boat, and how she then went below and put on a pea coat. Feeling satisfied that she had made herself safe from his molestation, she returned to him only to have him put his hands under the pea coat. She laughs at the naivete of herself as a child. We all laugh at the pain of her lost innocence with tears in our eyes.

I look and listen for laughter. Especially when I find myself feeling very grim, I open to the awareness that I may need to tune in to a channel on which I can laugh.

*Procrastination is born of my fear of beginning
or ending something. I ask for guidance to walk
through the fear.*

My childhood provided me with little reassurance that everything would be all right; instead
the impression of impending catastrophe was repeatedly confirmed. No wonder I became fearful
and tried to create a safe environment for myself
by choosing paths with fewer risks.

In recovery I recognize that I often procrastinate in areas where I fear the change of moving
on. I may want to quit my job, change careers, or
bring a long-term project to completion, but feel
paralyzed when it comes to action. I may put myself down as a slouch for procrastinating. It will
be more constructive if I simply ask for guidance
about my fears and become quiet enough to receive it. I will then be relieved of projecting myself into the future and discover whatever
unfinished business lies in the present waiting for
my attention. As I attend to it, I will find myself
able to rise to any risk.

I have faith that I am being cared for by my higher power. Everything I truly need is provided for me today.

Today I can see that I have been taken care of, even in what seemed to be my most dire times. I am grateful to be alive. Often in my anger over my incest, I feel that my higher power must have abandoned me. "If there is a God," rails the child within me, "how could it have let this happen?" But when I look at the larger picture I see that during my times of desperation, either as a child or as an adult, someone did help me. It was the fifth-grade teacher who chose to draw out a quiet child, the friend who called at the right moment, the sibling who offered companionship. Sometimes nature—through the song of a bird or the consoling motion of waves at the seashore— carried me past what seemed impossible pain to relief and lighter feelings. If I imagine linking all these life-saving experiences in a chain, I can understand the idea of a power greater than myself.

If I link only the horror and confusion of the incest experiences, I become lost in darkness. On a bleak day I may slip into doing this, temporarily forgetting my faith, but a phone call to a loving friend or someone in my incest recovery group will restore it. Then I will, once again, begin to see more clearly.

It is time for me to enjoy the fruits of being real; I allow myself to show how I feel inside.

Many of us were trapped in horrific circumstances. We might have been raped nightly by our father, "protected" by a mother who pretended to see or hear no evil, and who also pretended we needed to be sheltered from anything ugly or sexual outside our home. If we survived such hypocrisy, is it any wonder we learned to mask how we felt inside?

As I heal I gradually learn that I can allow myself to be real. I can examine the various ways I devised to exit from or disguise my feelings. I begin to make reparations to myself by staying with my insides and letting whatever I feel show through. I practice in the mirror, taking a look at my anger, my sadness, my joy. It feels good to say good riddance to pretending. I grow stronger from allowing myself to be real.

*I embrace my anger as a signal, acknowledge
it, and then look beneath it to see what other
feeling it is protecting me from.*

I need to pay attention to my anger in the way
I would listen to the fire siren if I were a volun-
teer fire fighter in my small town. I would
become alert for the next bit of information. I
would guard myself from other distractions. I
might feel a rush of adrenaline, but I would not
fly out the door with it until I knew where I was
going.

Often when I feel a flare of anger, I dash to get
away from it. I try to pretend it isn't present, seek
justification for it, or begin to get squirrelly in my
body, wishing I could get out of it. I have these
reactions because anger was never validated in
my early life. I was told I shouldn't have it or
show it. It became unmanageable because I was
never shown ways to manage it.

Today I can learn to manage it. I can keep an
anger journal, using writing as a way to acknowledge my anger. Writing about it frees me to see
the other feelings beneath it. Usually I have been
hurt and the anger gave me some distance and
protection from the vulnerability.

I write a letter of amends to my inner child, letting her know I am truly sorry for her suffering.

My inner child is in need of reparations. Even if I have chosen to confront my perpetrator or perpetrators, I cannot control their response. No one may ever write the letter my inner child would like to receive. But I do not have to wait, hope for the unlikely, or experience the helplessness of being passive.

I sit quietly and become meditative. I ask my inner child to tell me what she would like to be told. I listen carefully to what I hear. Then I take out a piece of paper and write to her. I respond to everything she has expressed a need for— whether it is to be told she didn't cause the incest, or that she was a cute and innocent child, or that she would like to have more chances to play now to make up for how overly serious she had to be back then.

I give her unconditional love. I tell her I have always loved her, but more and more now I learn how to respect and stay true to my love for her.

*When I feel time is running out and I had
better start rushing, I remind myself to quiet
down, turn inward, and stay present.*

Time is a unit of reality, yet my perception of
its passage varies greatly. My anxiety barometer
sometimes taps in to speed it up or at other
times, to slow it down. Sometimes I feel powerless against the effects of my anxiety. I may have
been powerless in my childhood and sought to
manipulate time as an escape or defense, but I am
not powerless now. When time seems off, I will
remember the tools I've learned for bringing myself to the present.

If time speeds up before the end of a visit, a
vacation, or a day, I can practice looking at all
that I enjoyed and accomplished instead of
yearning for what I didn't do. I can learn to trust
that I have followed the priorities that are right
for me at the moment. If there is something yet to
be done that I have pushed aside, I will let it
come to the forefront and attend to it. When I am
truly in the present, time will hold the comfort of
reality for me.

I have the opportunity to awaken fully to life regardless of my past.

Often when we have been abused in childhood we carry with us the despairing idea that we cannot escape the cycle of repeated abuse. That just as we begin to make some progress away from the old voices that oppress us, we will be snared as if by a lasso and thrown back onto the old ground. This thinking pattern can be so convincing within us that we constantly recreate a reality that confirms it. We would not want to describe ourselves as being comforted by this despair, yet we do not understand fully what binds us to a system in which the only reward is familiarity.

Risking belief in the possibility of my healing from the abuse is a first step in my exit from the constraints of the past. It is frightening to open to new experience and keep hope alive in the midst of it. This is the opportunity life presents me. With the help of my higher power I am strong enough to take it.

I am entitled to intimacy and am prepared to show up for it even if I must struggle to stay present.

To prepare myself for an intimate relationship, I start by developing a closer, more responsive connection with myself, then by building faith in the guidance of my higher power. My ability to trust grows slowly. It was shattered by the incest and now needs the sort of careful tending a newborn baby needs.

In a relationship, intimacy grows as two people encounter both their common ground and their areas of difference, some of which may arouse conflict. I must learn to exist with the presence of conflict and acquire and practice using tools for negotiation and resolution. Only then can I see that my whole self may exist intact even in a relationship. I can need and be needed without fearing annihilation. I can compromise after knowing I've been heard and my point of view understood. Each conflict walked through and resolved deepens my knowledge of myself and the other person.

I will not try to resolve everything at once, only one thing at a time, which makes life manageable.

Today I will open myself for intimacy by keeping what feels like the right distance from others for myself.

When someone stands too close to me, I feel discomfort and try to signal them to keep an appropriate distance. Or I create it myself by backing away. Emotionally, too, I require a certain amount of distance to feel safe and be open. I am entitled to my own comfort, and it is okay to declare my needs as they are. Otherwise, I will not be able to achieve intimacy.

In my family of origin, I was given the impression that being in the soup together, without any clear distinction of who was who, was the hallmark of intimacy. Today I know this is not true, and re-creating such a situation will only serve to make me feel victimized.

Intimacy requires having boundaries, but keeping them permeable so that love can pass in and out. I am in charge of the gate. If I hand that power over, even to a benevolent person, I will not be taking full responsibility for myself. I will be at risk and will not feel safe.

*To have new and different experiences, I must
first develop some faith in my new beliefs.*

Our thinking about who we are and what we
want plays a major part in creating our reality.
We may be full of wishful thinking: "If only my
work was noticed and appreciated. . . ." "If only I
had a partner who believed in me and nurtured
me. . . ." We convince ourselves that the very
strength of our wishes can create the reality we
desire. When we are disappointed that our
dreams aren't materializing, perhaps we need to
take some actions to make them materialize.

Do I really believe I am a valuable, worthy person who deserves to have my work noticed and
applauded? Am I ready to receive the nurturing
love of a partner? Have I begun to build a foundation around these beliefs? For instance, have I
learned to notice the many sources of love and
nurturing I encounter daily? Have I learned to let
these count? Have I learned to intercept thoughts
of worthlessness, or do I catch myself welcoming
their familiarity as if to say, of course you belong
here? I start where I am, laying brick and mortar.
I have the materials in hand.

*I flourish with creativity, opening to the flow of
my spirit.*

My creative spirit remained whole even when I
moved so far away from it that it felt unreal or
disconnected from me. It was the part of me that
held fast to the Great Mother's ground and knew
that my imagination sprouted truth. It was the
part that believed in the notion of spring, of re-
birth and transformation, even in my darkest
hour. In my lowest moments it sowed seeds from
which new life could grow.

Because of the power this creative spirit has to
heal me, I've always heard voices telling me to
stay away from it. They say, "Who do you think
you are? . . ." "Who wants to hear you express
yourself? . . ." "What makes you think you're so
special?"

We are each very special and have been given
creative gifts to use for expressing and connecting
with our spirit. I will let myself flourish with the
use of this transforming power and leave those
whimpering voices to complain without effect.

My spirit ascends each time I realize I am making myself whole.

We journey downward to discover the dark truths that have been buried in us and hidden from us. Like Inanna in the Sumerian myth, we are stripped of old trappings as we go so that we arrive in the underworld naked and vulnerable. It may feel as if we will never be able to get out, as if this is our final destination. We cry out for help. Inanna's help came in the form of two humble creatures made of bits of dirt who responded to her cries with empathy and were then able to negotiate for her freedom.

To gain maturity I need to become acquainted with all aspects of myself. Each time I make a descent, I strip away another level of illusion that has kept me living with counterfeit notions. I return with greater ease because of self-knowledge, ascending with a deeper knowledge of myself, realizing to enter my darkness allows me to see my light shine brighter.

*My body houses my life; I respect and care for
it to the best of my ability.*

Many of us who have survived abuse find ourselves strapped with a legacy of neglect to our
body. Long after the abuser is out of the scene, we
continue to perpetuate this negligence. We may
be frightened of doctors, deny or split off from
warning signals of pain and fatigue, feel ashamed
of being ill or having accidents. Even if we are
secretly grateful when a breakdown of our body
expresses our hurt, acting out a negligent relationship to our body still leaves us feeling like a
victim.

Today in recovery I have another choice. I
choose to consciously love and care for my body.
I can search until I find capable and caring doctors, dentists, or other caretakers with whom I
feel comfortable. I can tune into my body both in
sickness and in health, respect its limitations, and
take fine care of it. I can nurture myself with the
gifts of regular exercise, hearty nourishment, and
restful sleep. I can care for the needs of my body
promptly each day, realizing procrastination is
likely to harm me.

Even when I cannot see my own progress, I persevere by staying present and taking heart from seeing the progress my sister survivors are making.

Once we are out of denial, we are on our way to recovery. We often start with a rush of energy that had been held out of reach by our denial. We surge forward with glimpses of being liberated from the role of victim long ago laid down like a blueprint in our heads.

The nature of my recovery is hard to perceive correctly from inside myself alone. I experience myself moving awkwardly forward in fits and starts, and often stalling as if I am out of gas. I become easily discouraged and subject to the notion that all my efforts are for naught—that my past has entrapped me and is not going to let me go.

At these times, being in a group with other incest survivors can be the key to recharging my hope. As I note how others work through their problems, I can see with confidence that they are moving, even when their own perceptions may arouse the feeling that they are standing still. When someone in my group has a victory, it feels like a victory for all of us, and is. I can see all the struggle that led up to the victory. I allow her healing to be my healing.

*I value and honor the way my suffering brings
me to further search and surrender.*

In deep despair I feel there is no place to turn.
I want out. I am not sure out of what. I may have
ideas of suicide or wish to leave a situation I feel
is making me feel too vulnerable to further injury. I may yearn to fill myself up with addictive
behaviors or substances that I have committed to
refrain from. I feel empty, unfilled, and yet if I
take a clear look, I *am filled,* only with pain.

Each of us has moments like this. I do not
need to fear I am going crazy. I do not need to
fear I will stay this way forever. I need to embrace
and accept my pain. Sometimes I need to share it
with people who are empathetic. Often in the
deepest depths of despair, I will find myself able
to call out without qualification for my higher
power's help. A light will then begin to shine and
lead me back out of the abyss.

Today I do not need to be controlled by my fear.

Sometimes I feel afraid without understanding what is happening to me or why. It may not help to try to analyze; it may only make me feel more stymied. At times like this, I need only do my best to keep showing up in the places where I am most able to be myself. In a meeting of sexual abuse survivors I heard someone say, "My incest is bothering me today." That was all she needed to know. She had shown up and knew she would be okay.

When my incest is bothering me, I feel like a victim. I feel as if everyone wants to control my life, and as if I am not in charge of what I want and need or even how to make my wants and needs known. I feel as if I am losing my freedom. When I feel this way inside, I am likely to start arguments or try to find someone or something to blame. A moment of quiet attention to my inner child can help me. Perhaps reflecting on the notion that I can receive guidance from my higher power. Perhaps making an effort to help someone else for a moment, or reminding myself of all I have accomplished in healing from my incest experience. Any of these ways can take me out of darkness and toward the light.

I recognize the depth of betrayal and the trauma of my sexual abuse so that I can heal from it.

A seven-year-old girl trusts and emulates her sixteen-year-old brother. When on vacation at the shore, he invites her to come into the deep water with him. Of course she goes eagerly. How could she possibly know that once out over her head, he is going to pull her bathing suit aside and stick his penis in her while she clutches desperately to him to keep from drowning? How will she ever recover from this trauma?

Sometimes another's story can seem more traumatic than our own. But we each have a story of deep betrayal. I must recognize the extent of my own trauma and weep for the child who endured it. She had great hopes for loving attention from the person who abused her. Her very eagerness made her vulnerable. She was put into shock by the traumatic events, and has since had many of the symptoms now known as post-traumatic stress syndrome. Giving this trauma full recognition is an act of love and a first step toward healing.

I distinguish vulnerability from passivity and realize I can be vulnerable without becoming a victim.

We each have a wide range of being—from an active and assertive state to a more passive and receptive state. To allow myself vulnerability requires that I move toward the more receptive state. And in doing this I easily become confused and fearful that I can experience this part of myself only by becoming a victim. I must learn to make some distinctions.

The passive receptive mode is crucial to going inside, deepening my understanding of myself, and allowing myself to heal. I can call on my higher power to help me feel safe there. It may feel as if I am entering strange and scary territory, for in the past I have clung to control even when it meant deprivation. But as I release the tight fist of control, I appreciate the inner wealth that has long been awaiting my ability to receive it.

I will not tolerate battering under any circumstances.

Because of the abuse I suffered in the past, I am likely to feel confused even now if I find myself in a battering situation. If another person tells me I am the cause of their anger or accuses me of provoking them, I am susceptible to having my shame buttons pushed and believing them. Just because I have this reaction does not make their accusations true. My reaction is an outgrowth of having been blamed as a child.

No one deserves to be battered. I have the freedom to exit any situation that I feel is physically or emotionally battering. I do not need the other person to agree with me that this is what is going on. I can stand on my own judgment and seek the assistance and support necessary to guide me to a place where I feel safe.

Each time I enter my body more fully, I birth myself to a greater awakening.

We all have areas of our body we experience acutely and other areas that seem numb, hardly present, or that we become aware of only through pain. Incest survivors are especially likely to have absented themselves from parts of their body. And we might continue for years without even a sense of what we were missing. People may generally believe it is difficult to be out of the body, but for us it may be more difficult to be in it.

In my healing I gradually reclaim my whole body. To do so I need to gently enter each area I have blocked off to sensation. I may feel ecstatic when I do this or I may feel clobbered with pain. Regardless of the sensation, I am grateful for the ability to feel what was previously unfelt. I practice releasing any judgments I might make of my experience and welcome and greet each new area of my body that is ready to be enlivened— whether it is an eye that was formerly unseeing or the soles of my feet that now feel the sensation of the ground.

Rage is resourcelessness. I have rage but I also have resources to call upon to help me not displace it.

Once I let myself digest the horror I feel at my memories, I am likely to become outraged at what I endured as a child. Looking at my own children or the children of others, I see just how vulnerable and tender we are at certain ages, and how a direct expression of my anger was not possible at the time. It was shunned by the perpetrator, I was punished for exhibiting anger, or I was threatened with the loss of a contact that contained the possibility of love.

I am both outraged and in rage at what happened to me. Once my rage is let out, it may spew like a volcano. It may threaten to spill over into my relationships, especially the intimate ones. Anyone close may feel threatening to me and provoke my fiery feelings.

I remind myself today that I have resources to address my rage. I can beat on pillows and scream it out. I can share it with my therapist. Instead of injuring my loved ones with it, I can hold myself, see myself in a mirror, and assure myself that I am ever-moving toward the life that has been buried under these stuffed feelings.

I respect the fear I feel before a visit with my family. It warns me to prepare by reinforcing ways to stay true to my recovering self.

Return visits to my family have often been devastating events. Pulled in by the undertow of the past, I ended up feeling as small and beached on a lone shore as I had been as a child. Despite the pain of these visits, I often gained insights and saw my family more clearly after the experience.

Today I do not need to suffer revictimization when I visit with my family, but I do need to prepare myself and not trivialize the potency of these visits. I prepare by staying close to the protection of my higher power through daily prayer and meditation. I remind myself that I have the resources and tools of my recovery and use them as needed throughout the visit. For instance, I may excuse myself during the visit to call someone who knows how I have been troubled by my relationship to my family. I reassure my inner child that I am aware of her need for protection and use the visit as an opportunity to develop my skill for nurturing myself. Rather than protecting others in the family from responsibility for their behavior, I am vigilant in remaining loyal to myself.

I affirm my ability and right to treat my inner child with compassion.

Years of neglectful and abusive treatment by a parent and other authority figures left my inner child cowering in a corner, hoping to escape notice. As I recover, she will gradually come out in the light, albeit fearfully. I can and will learn to protect and defend her, to create a safe space for her. Little by little she will learn to trust me if I steadfastly avoid treating her as she was treated in the past.

As I grow stronger in my confidence that I can protect her, I will be faced with the difficult task of feeling her pain and deep sorrow. I will cry for her. I will tell her I am sorry for the things that happened to her. I will give her reassurance, hold and rock her, and recognize her as the wounded part of me. I will look in the mirror and touch her face. I will promise her my loyalty. If I veer from providing this, I will make amends as soon as I become aware of my error, forgive myself, and begin again to become trustworthy to her. Even when I fail, I will not have abandoned my commitment to love her.

My first reaction to breaking silence is to quake. Then I know I have created room in which to grow.

Whether implicit or explicit, we who've been sexually abused have been given the message to shut up about it. Misplaced shame has been used to silence us. Threats have been rained on our needs. We have dreams of telling and then being mutilated for it. We have memories of telling and being ridiculed or ignored. We have built our silence around us as a fortress to protect us. It should not surprise us then that it is not easy to break it.

I tell first the people who are safest—other survivors, a trusted therapist, a close friend, possibly a lover. I experience the reverberations of my telling, how the fear of reprisal planted in my past contrasts with my present experience. Did I receive empathy and compassion when I expected to be told to shut up? Did my world expand when I feared telling would only lead me to further shame?

I do not need to tell all too soon or to tell everyone. I use judgment, pace myself, and wait to tell more when the time is right for me.

Fear does not stop me from changing, though it accompanies me.

Life is a dynamic force, ever-changing, yet I often yearn for it to be static—as if that would give me the control I think I need to feel secure and unafraid. I found ways of "stopping time" as a child when under attack. I went out of body, into a persona, or into a playroom in my imagination to ensure my survival. I respect how this creative adjustment of reality was an important tool for me, yet now I wish to grow and leave behind my old behaviors.

Of course I will feel fear as I do so. I will feel as if I am removing an old familiar coat that has made me comfortable. I know little about the new way I am adopting. When fear comes, my mind may say I am not ready for change and must have made the wrong decision. But I will use my faith to balance my mind. For I know this is my path and that my discomfort is a natural part of walking into unfamiliar territory. If I panic, I will slow down and take the time to acknowledge and work with my fears so that I will be able to go on with all of me intact.

*I trust myself to integrate and use all I have
learned in a way that benefits me.*

A common coping mechanism of sexual abuse
victims is to split off to get at least partially away
from the abuse experience. Sometimes, even
many years after the abuse, we remain split in
various ways. One of these may be that it is difficult for us to believe that we have developed
into a competent and capable adult who can protect us and behave in ways that carry us effectively into the world. If we chart what that adult
has done, we will realize we have taken her to
therapists and groups where she has learned
many new ways that were not taught in our families. She may have gone to school and earned di-
plomas and degrees. Still, when we are under
stress and revert to feeling as we did when we
were abandoned as children, we may find it hard
to believe there is anyone who can rescue us.

In my recovery I learn to trust and utilize my
adult self as a protector. I let the sum total of my
experience count. I spent many years indoctrinated
in the ways of my family but I have also spent much
time away from them, receptive to the ways of healing. I integrate and use them now.

I seek the clarity of accurate perception before I am ready for action.

More often than I experience clarity, I experience being fogged in with confusion. I need to accept this as an interim state, one of some protection. I offer myself compassion in this state rather than listening to the negative voice that would have me dump on myself for being in the fog. My fogging out as a child may have served as a major defense for me. If I have fogged out in the past with alcohol or other drugs, I will be fearful of the way this state resembles these old experiences. But I am capable of making distinctions.

Today I have resources to bring me gradually back to clarity. I have learned that it is helpful to share my feelings and problems with others who understand them and are willing to listen caringly. I know how to seek guidance from my higher power. I do not need to rush to relieve discomfort, but must sit quietly with myself until I firmly connect with both my adult and my inner child. When I am not quite ready to let go, there is likely to be a foggy atmosphere. But as I come into myself more strongly, the fog lifts and I am shown the way to go.

Today I am grateful to have found a road to recovery.

At times the recovery road seems almost too rutted to travel, yet I realize every step of progress has brought me into myself. By gradually restoring my memories, I am coming to own my experience and thereby giving myself new life. I need not feel ashamed of myself for the incest experience. And as I let go of shame, I am able to treat the child within me with love and compassion. Each time I do this, I grow more substantial and whole.

Recovery is painful but joyful. I know there are many incest survivors who still suffer and have not yet found a supportive place in which to begin this journey. There are many who are beginning their recovery by first achieving sobriety or abstinence from drugs or other addictions. I am grateful to have found resources—survivors with like injury and literature that describes and documents our problems. I recognize that my recovery can help others, just as others have helped me. I reach out when possible.

February

*I check myself against scapegoating others and
do not need to serve as a scapegoat for anyone.*

We each have our light and dark sides. Carl
Jung named the dark side of the psyche the
shadow. When we are unable or unwilling to
own all aspects of ourselves, we tend to split the
light side from the dark side and project the dark
side onto someone or something else.

My dark side contains feelings of rage, guilt,
and shame about the abuse. My abuser tried to
pass these negative feelings over to me by abusing me, and in my resentment against this I may
feel justified in not owning my shadow but finding someone else to push it onto. For example,
when I am hurting it may be easier for me to
think someone is hurting me than to simply say I
am hurting. But try as I might, this will not be
satisfying.

To be whole is my vision and the way to my healing. I can only achieve this solid state of being by
owning every aspect of me. I learn to identify when
I am attempting to use someone else as a scapegoat
to escape my feelings. Then I return the focus to
myself. I also learn to keep a clear boundary to protect myself from being used by others who might
seek a scapegoat as my abuser did.

If I choose to confront my perpetrator, I recognize this is an action I am doing only for myself.

Confrontation is one of the tools of healing. It is not an end point or final goal to be accomplished so that I will be finished with my whole ordeal. I need to place it in perspective with the other recovery tools I am learning to use daily.

As survivors of abuse—people whose needs were not seriously given consideration and satisfaction—we are likely to have attitudes that make us want to act quickly for immediate gratification. In the beginning of healing from the abuse, as anger flares up into rage, many of us are attracted to the idea of rushing to confront the perpetrator. We are wisely counseled to slow down and think through our motives for confrontation and our readiness to let go of the outcome of the confrontation.

When I am truly ready, I will see how my confrontation is an action I do solely for myself. I will arrange the situation in a way that protects me, and I will not overly concern myself with the effects on the perpetrator.

I respect the wisdom and knowledge that is stored in my body. I no longer want to reject or disown my body.

Often when I suffer from an injury or an illness, I get the sense that my body is attempting to express a vulnerability that I am unable to express in any other way. It is as if my body is forcing me to slow down to care for my wounds.

Particularly when I am making major changes, I am likely to try to exit from my feelings. Then the integrity of my body steps in. In the past I blocked awareness of this through the use of alcohol or other drugs. Now I can begin to appreciate my body as a friend.

It is difficult to encounter memories that have been blocked from the mind but contained in the body, and to realize that others may still be buried. But today I learn to trust the storage of these memories and the timing of their release as I grow strong enough to receive them. This is a gift from my higher power. Some memories come in dreams, some are sparked by hearing others' stories, some are lodged in body positions or postures. They come when I am ready to deal with them.

My sense of self-worth grows from the enthusiastic response I give to myself today.

Children learn to value themselves through being valued by others, particularly their parents. Those of us who grew up in families where we were not valued started down one, believing we were not only not valued but unworthy and bad, less than zero. Consequently, the good things that happen to us we tend to discount because they don't match this inner belief in our badness. When we needed enthusiastic appraisal and encouragement to thrive, we received poisonous barbs, criticism, beatings, and invasions of our body. Or we were systematically ignored and withdrawn from, a treatment just as cruel as negative attention or more overt abuse.

Today I can reparent myself in a way that builds self-esteem. I am diligent in my efforts to treat myself consistently with high regard. This means breaking with the old abusive messages that are so familiar they almost seem comforting. I notice my achievements, refuse to cut off and ignore my feelings, and stop whenever I feel down on myself because of where I am. I begin again to wrap myself in the love I have spent years lacking.

*As I go through changes, I notice how much
more readily I see gifts and opportunities than
I did before beginning to heal.*

Change is not easy for us. We want something
to hold steady. We have difficulty reconciling
with the notion that all life is dynamic and that
things change. Much of our pain comes from our
resistance. "Oh, please, please, don't let this be
so," we plead when we've been given information
we know will have to be absorbed. We may have
started crying out like this at the time of our
abuse, hoping that we could put up a shield that
would let us cling to the sense of safety we had
before.

In my healing I realize I can turn my forces to
being a participant in change rather than a resis-
ter to it. I discard old notions of how long a
change will require me to suffer. I discover there
is excitement in change that I no longer need to
push away. I remain present for my life today and
look forward to and appreciate change as part of
my unfolding.

*I am building a healthy support system and
learning to use it readily.*

Many of us have lived in severe isolation for
most of our life. We've thought the only way to
safety was to learn to do virtually everything
alone. We've focused less on developing relationships and more on trying to consolidate our
strength and being able to ward off anything that
would hurt us.

In our healing we learn that we need others. We
are interdependent people coexisting on this
planet. It would be an unnatural goal to strive for
total self-sufficiency. We need to recruit people who
can help us, making sure that they are trustworthy.

I establish relationships with a good therapist, a
support group of other abuse survivors, and a few
good friends. It is one thing to build this network,
another to use it. I must reach out both when I feel
good and when I am in pain. The latter may be
hardest, but I will discover that others have a readiness to hear me, that I am no longer surrounded by
people who deny feelings, and that my sharing less-
ens the weight of my burdens.

I accept and love myself exactly as I am today; I build my foundation for growth out of acceptance.

Because of the neglect I suffered in my background, I often feel ill-equipped for life. But rather than be discouraged, I am learning to find the resources to help me participate fully in the world, to make choices to take care of myself, to enjoy relationships. Often my individual needs and the needs of a relationship will appear to conflict. I can do my best to stay in charge of my own needs rather than feeling guilty for having them.

It is important to remember that though I make mistakes, I am not a mistake. I am merely a person making an effort to act for myself and achieve balance in all realms. I acknowledge my progress. I recognize perfectionism as potentially self-abusive and as a mode that has often paralyzed me in the past. If I am tempted to succumb to feelings of failure, I stop and take a close look to see that there is progress in the fact that I am making an effort. I credit myself for this and accept myself wherever I am on my journey instead of expecting or wishing to be someplace else.

I become a student in self-trust. I learn to doubt myself without getting stuck in doubt.

I grew up having to discount my intuitions and feelings. Rather than being encouraged to trust myself, I was told to believe I should and could only trust those in authority. If they said they loved me, then surely that must be what love was.

Today I begin anew to study trust. I take my intuitions and feelings as the building blocks. Yet I recognize that my perceptions are often distorted by looking through the lens of the past. If I am in a situation in which I feel uncertain, I do not need to shame myself and rush to a place of greater knowing. A certain amount of self-doubt is healthy. For instance, if I have recently undergone a major loss, such as the death of a parent, I may have acute feelings of abandonment that lead me to see the loss around every corner. On the other hand, I may be having an accurate perception. Because when my feelings are mixed, I have no way of knowing I need to wait until I can see a clearer picture. I can be in doubt as long as I need to be without being stuck there.

I release the old habit of hasty decision making and allow my decisions to evolve and emerge in harmony with my higher power's time.

Because I was given few lessons in independence or self-care in my abusive childhood, it is difficult for me now to make balanced decisions. But I am capable of learning this skill.

In the past I may have acted too quickly because I needed to get away from uncomfortable feelings. If I was half in, half out of a relationship, I felt I had to decide at once which way to go. I didn't stop to ask the question: Why am I half in, half out? Am I frightened of the commitment? Am I hesitant because I'm not feeling loved? I raced on to make a decision that often left out some part of me. Then I lurched sufferingly along as if one of my legs was dragging behind me.

Today I know I can make balanced decisions by giving myself time, receiving counsel from my therapist and others I trust, and feeling the feelings that arise. When I feel 50/50 about something, I need to go on exploring and adding new information until I come to 70/30 or 20/80. When it is time, my decision will feel as if it has grown out of me. And whatever loss accompanies it, I can accept because I will be fully present in the process.

*Today I understand that I need not be ashamed
to speak openly about incest.*

I no longer need to fear reprisal from the perpetrators of the abuse I suffered, nor do I care to
seek their approval or attention. I was made mute
by the incest experience. I stuffed my feelings
and protected the perpetrators by silencing myself. Then this was crucial for my survival. Now I
have love and compassion for the child in me
who was able to adapt to the circumstances and
find the right mechanisms to carry me through.
Now I have created the space, through my healing, to live a life that goes beyond survival. Mute-
ness only conceals my feelings and makes me feel
small.

I began by speaking out in safe places—where
I was likely to be among peers who shared my experience or with a trusted therapist. Over time I
grew stronger, and today I am able to speak out
publicly. I will no longer pretend that there is
something wrong with me when there is not. My
silence was something designed to protect the
perpetrator.

*When weary I will take time to create the right
conditions to replenish myself.*

Especially because I often behave or think
obsessively—a mode I use to escape thoughts or
memories of the abuse—I often become weary
and depleted. I dread feeling this way because it
means I have to stop my motor and put myself in
neutral. And I fear I will then be plagued by my
woundedness. But going on and on in this way is
harmful and will ultimately lead me to illness, injury, or some other event that will bring me to a
halt.

I can stop and rest. I can even consciously
determine that I want to give myself a time-out
from my incest recovery. I will not return to
denial if I put what I've learned on the shelf
for a little while to let myself lighten up, regain
composure, and experiment with other ways of
living.

I also focus on learning day by day to take the
rest I need to restore my energy. I recognize my
limitations and the fact that it is perfectly normal
to become tired. I learn to create conditions con-
ducive for replenishing myself and allow myself
to use them.

*I express myself to the spirit of my perpetrator
who is dead and believe I am heard.*

It is important for those of us who have been
victimized by so much else not to fall victim to
the idea that since our perpetrator is dead, we
will never have a chance to confront him or her.
Though it will not be the same type of confrontation, we can confront spirit to spirit and in doing so alter our relationship to that figure.

Many incest survivors find it helpful to write a
letter to their perpetrator telling exactly what
their experiences were, telling the person how he
or she hurt them, and expressing what their inner child would like to receive in the way of
amends. Others use visualization and tell the perpetrator out loud about these things.

I choose the way that feels right for me and
pursue it. I might light a candle, call the spirit of
my father, and begin a conversation that will take
place over several sessions. I might have one or
more of my sister survivors present as a witness. I
might create a ritual with the help of my therapist. As I try out each new possibility, I discover
what works to empower me.

*I will dare to take the risks necessary to have
the good life I want and deserve to have.*

It is tough to take risks, especially if my modus
operandi as a child was to crawl under the table
to disappear when things proved dangerous to
me. But today I am an adult with some control
over my life. I do not need to be subject to anyone's tyranny. I am free to make the choices that
suit me. I do not need to restrict myself to a small
world in order to create safety.

Often, in order to have what we want and deserve, we must risk closing one door without
knowing where or when another will open. This
might mean leaving an abusive relationship or a job
that is draining us. It might mean saying no to playing our old role in our family, or it might mean setting up new boundaries with our children.

We may fear that if we attempt change there
will be nothing for us. It is then we need to trust
that our higher power will guide us even if we
feel lost. We will be amazed to discover that no
sooner have we accepted our situation than new
doors begin to open. What seemed like great risk
was only the unknown.

I am learning to confront abuse whenever I encounter it, and I will be capable of confronting my past abusers if and when it feels vital to my recovery.

Each of us must determine if, how, and when to confront our abusers. I might desire to do so as a way of handing over responsibility I wrongly absorbed long ago, because I want to break the secret, or because I want to verify to my inner child my belief in her experience.

There are different ways to confront. I may choose to alter my relationship with the perpetrator by letting that person know I will not tolerate treatment that implies subordination. I can temporarily retreat from my family, explaining only as much as I wish to. For instance, I can say, "It is not good for me to be in contact with you now while I am looking at my childhood."

If I decide to confront specifically about the abuse, I will prepare myself beforehand so that I do not injure myself further with an act meant to heal me. I can read the literature about this, speak to others who have done it, and establish a network of people ready and able to support me.

I value myself today from within and do not plummet or rise according to the reflection of others.

As a child I was dependent on the reflection of my parents for a sense of self-worth, but they were not able to supply reliable positive feedback. They were bound by their own shame and eager to pass it on to someone less powerful. When I should have been getting a sense of my innate worthiness, I was receiving instead the message that something was wrong with me, that I was trouble or a nuisance, or "too big for my britches."

In recovery my self-worth becomes apparent to me. Yet it grows slowly, is fragile, and is subject to falling apart from time to time—a phenomenon common to being human. I develop an awareness of taking responsibility for holding my value within instead of turning it over to other people—an employer, a lover, a friend. If I am offered a job that doubles my income, I am likely to believe this raise increases my value, but even here I need to stay steady with my inner value. I am much more than a job.

Detachment can help me center myself and give me a balanced view of myself separate from others.

In close relationships it is very easy to lose track of where I end and the other begins. The needs of two people become closely intertwined when there is mutual caring, but in my incestuous family there was little or no respect taught for boundaries. Thus, I need to start from scratch to become clear about who I am and where I begin and end as I enter into and periodically as I continue a relationship.

Detachment is a helpful skill in which I consciously turn the focus back onto myself. I realize my concern for the other person's needs, but my primary responsibility is to myself. If I discover that I've eased off my vigilance and let someone leave some of their garbage in my lap, I need to stand up and hand it back as kindly as possible When I have returned to carrying my own burdens and truly believing it is okay that I do only that, I will have achieved detachment. I will be able to express myself honestly and allow outcomes to be out of my hands.

I was powerless over the incest experience and I will accept the freedom from guilt and shame this knowledge offers me.

I was forced to keep the secret of the incest in my family. At some point the secrecy translated into a feeling of having some control over things. But what an illusion and burden that was.

It is a relief now to realize I was powerless over the experience. I no longer need to grasp at secrecy as control. I can let go and concentrate my efforts on taking care of myself, attending to my wants and needs.

I cannot control the behavior of any other human being. Because of the abuse I received, I felt a strong need to get control over others. Today I can release the guilt and shame, and admit the ways in which my life was focused on trying to control others. I can redirect myself to taking care of my own business.

When I am humble I have my right-sized place in the world and know that I can be helped and help others.

Because of my history as an abuse survivor, my first reaction to the notion of humility is that it means victimization. In place of humility, I erected defenses to protect myself, including arrogance, grandiosity, and a distorted sense of myself as being in charge. It is not easy to lower these walls put up to protect a little girl, powerless over the abuse, who had no way to put what was happening into perspective. Now it is time to recognize that while these walls have protected me, they have also blocked the light from shining on my problems.

As I develop a growing faith in the existence of a power greater than myself, I experience the humility of how much I don't know. I can see that I am a person among people, a unique, important, and precious human being, yet one who does not need to be elevated above others to be respected. As I allow myself to be human, I become patient with myself in my process. My tolerance for the limitations of others grows too, along with my ability to extend a helping hand and to ask for one.

I refrain from trivializing the covert abuse
I suffered and allow myself to assess its
damages.

Those of us whose sexual abuse occurred more in the emotional than the physical realm may find it harder to claim our woundedness. We may feel as if we have no right to complain when we hear stories of ritual abuse or other outrageous acts such as out-and-out rape by relatives. But we hurt ourselves by comparing stories. For we each have but one story to begin with—our own story—and we need to comprehend how we were affected. Slanted glances at our developing bodies, being caught in a tangled emotional web between our parents, having our privacy invaded continually—all these can have very damaging results.

Today I practice identifying with others whose abuse was more overt, rather than using their experiences to dismiss my own. I assess my damages. When I do this I can better understand how often I have been paralyzed and unable to take good care of myself. I can recover by accepting my own story.

I take the appropriate amount of space, neither acting invisible nor becoming overbearing.

In my family of origin, I was not taught appropriate and respectful boundaries for taking up space. My own space was leveled by people with the authority to get away with it. No apologies or amends were made to me for being overrun. It was as if I didn't exist or didn't matter.

Today I know that I matter. I also know that I come with problems in this area and must bring myself up anew with some gentle and rational guidance. I may intuitively know the appropriate place to put my boundaries, but I will not always be free enough from threatening feelings to tap my intuition. Or I may be up against someone else's aggression that reminds me of the ways I was obliterated in the past.

When the time is right for me, I take the space that is mine. Steadfast and sturdy, I stand for what is mine.

Painful as flashbacks are, I recognize them as opportunities to gain greater clarity by returning to experiences that were clouded and muffled.

We are given the ability to split off at least some parts of ourselves for self-protection at times of great distress or shocking trauma. This allows us to go through difficult experiences without any feeling. Consequently, we might have amnesia about certain events or even about long periods of our childhood.

As I break the silence about the abuse I received and build a support system of others who hear and understand me, I begin to heal and become ready to work with the flashbacks I have. They come as clear memories or as overwhelming floods of feeling aroused by a sight, smell, or someone's touch, seeing a child treated abusively, or seeing someone in a helpless condition.

When I have a flashback, I remind myself that I am an adult who can work through it. I stay with the feelings, knowing I am not doing this to punish myself but to allow a reclaiming of my experience that makes me sturdy and contributes to my healing.

When I have recognized the things I can change and have had the courage to do my footwork, I will find serenity quietly sailing into my mind.

So often what takes the place of serenity in our minds is the constant chatter of internal conflict. We have internalized the voices of our parents and other authority figures. Each time we act or make a statement that aligns us with ourselves, we are likely to set off those voices. They tell us that we are unworthy, stupid, inadequate, ill-prepared, or setting ourselves up for a fall.

I work by taking one step at a time to change the things I can. When I have made a movement in a good direction and am still besieged by inner torment, I will not interpret my discomfort to mean I have taken the wrong initiative. I will look to the next piece of footwork and take strength from my relationship to a higher power. When I have done all that I can and know it is time to turn the rest over to my higher power, I will be amazed at the silence that will settle inside me. Such peace restores me.

I want each of my relationships to be a dialogue in which there is a continual unfolding of myself and the other person.

Healthy relationships are dialogues. The out-of-sync times lead to new and deeper understandings. I negotiate for my present needs with someone who has her or his own needs. Even if we come up with a solution or strategy, we will be wise to recognize that our individual needs are always changing and nothing has to remain rigid.

In my abusive family there was no dialogue. There were the monologues of the authority figures. There was the silence or the acting out of those of us who felt we were being controlled. Efforts we made to reach through the fog to be recognized were not received constructively but were struck down.

Today I am prone to feeling controlled in my relationships, but I must recognize I have the freedom to leave. I have the freedom to speak and the right to be heard. Learning to partake of and create a respectful system in my relationships will not come overnight, but I am equipped with the tools to work at it.

Today I will recognize anger as an emotion that can protect me.

When my cat is threatened, I notice that the hair on her back stands up, her eyes open wide, and she makes a noise that says, "Don't come too close to me." I was powerless over my incest experience, and while I felt anger, I was told by someone more powerful than me not to express it. When I displayed it anyway, I was punished for that. So I learned to express it in roundabout ways. Or I turned it on the only one safe enough to turn it on—myself.

Today I realize I am entitled to own my anger and I use it for my protection. I do not want to abuse others with it, nor do I want to abuse myself with it. But when I suppress it, it saps my energy—the same energy I need to go forth boldly and take my God-given space in the world. I shall learn ways to express it directly and effectively.

At low moments, when I feel I have reached the bottom of my well of inspiration and do not know where to turn, I find myself led by my higher power.

Inspiration comes from many sources. It conveys hope. I might find inspiration in someone's writing, in spoken conversation, in the movement of a dancer, in a painting, in the beauty of a baby. Although these are many sources of inspiration, perhaps they are only one — the higher power's expression of truth beaming through on multiple channels.

When I feel as if my well is dry and there is nothing to tap inside me, I can look outside. I was frightened to do this as a child because it seemed safer to remain isolated and rely only on myself. But now I am capable of choosing safe places and reaching out to others.

I can put myself in a receptive mode and allow the hope of others to fill my well. They are my fellow human beings and may provide for me today and receive from me tomorrow.

*I regret the abuse I suffered, yet I value the way
healing from it has deepened me.*

All human beings, whether survivors of childhood abuse or not, are confronted with illness,
accidents, loss of loved ones, and a whole host of
other injuries that hurt us and we wish hadn't
happened. Yet don't we learn from these times
how to value what we may have taken for
granted—good health, for instance? And don't
we discover resources that might have otherwise
lain dormant in us?

As I deal with my memories of abuse, I often rail
against my lot, wishing this history belonged to
someone else, that I could be free from it. But then
I wonder, who would this someone else be? I realize
how much strength I've observed in myself as I've
grappled with my pain. I've found the me who
came through. I've found the freedom to leave behind more superficial masks that otherwise might
have covered my face for a lifetime.

When I recognize I am powerless over my feelings, I can turn them over to a power greater than myself.

There is no greater quandary than admitting I am powerless when everything is so messy and disorderly inside me that it seems as if I should struggle to grasp at any power I can get. But this is exactly when I have learned that what will help me is surrender, not clinging to my last illusion of power.

As a child no one walked me through my feelings. No one told me they would pass. No one told me I was more than the sum of those feelings. Instead, I was encouraged to stuff them. They were pushed away as inconvenient or perceived as threatening. I may have even been punished for having them.

Today I do not punish myself for having feelings. I welcome them. I also recognize in times of intense feelings that I need help to move through them. This is when I reach out for the help of my higher power, either through people who support me or through prayer and meditation. If I am open, I will receive the help I need.

I envision myself as healthy and healing.

To move from one way of being to another requires vision. I do not dare divest myself of old trappings if I believe this will leave me naked and with nothing to protect myself. But by allowing myself a vision of the new way, I create a path to move along and do not need to feel as if change means I will be exposed in a way that will harm me.

This envisioning may be difficult at first. In the abusive times of my childhood I did not have a way out. I was hopelessly trapped. I used my imagination to create escapes for self-preservation, yet I was unable to remove my body from the uncomfortable circumstances. I need to now distinguish between using my imagination to escape and using it to create a belief system in a new way of life.

To even say the words out loud—"I envision myself healthy and healing"—can be intimidating, for it is a type of empowerment that the negative voices in me discourage. I will make a practice of repeatedly speaking my visions and note with awe when they begin to come true.

I am reclaiming myself from the missing persons list.

As an incest survivor I can readily identify with the person born on February 29 who must borrow someone else's birthday three out of every four years. What a calamitous fate, I cry out. It's not fair. Even the calendar is not 100 percent reliable.

When we were victimized as children, we may have felt like a missing person. Either we went numb and then felt missing to ourselves, or we couldn't understand how we could be having the experience we were having. It seemed as if our higher power had deserted us or couldn't see us. Or our parent who we relied on to see us was using us instead of seeing us.

Today I reclaim myself from the missing persons list. I am present here and now and I count on myself to show up. When the missing persons feelings creep up on me, I see them for what they are—flashbacks to moments of neglect in my childhood. I take care to embrace myself more fully and remind myself I am alive and well, and no one can take that away from me.

March

I allow myself choices about sex that will contribute to my healing.

As we go through our recovery, sex can be difficult and tricky for those of us who are incest survivors. Some of us were promiscuous in the past, daring and bold and cavalier. Perhaps we even endangered ourselves, acting fearless and as if we needed some extra excitement to feel a high. As we move into recovery, we see how our attitudes were formed by our history as incest survivors. We recognize we were often not fully there for sex but somewhere out of body, or in a persona. Or we may have gone the opposite way and shied away from sex, yet felt deprived and lonely because of our remoteness.

Today I treat sex as a delicate matter. My feelings about it are tender and need to be respected and considered with that tenderness in mind. I often wish that I could make a giant leap to end up at the "normal" end of the continuum, by-passing all need for communication and adjusting to my feelings. But wouldn't this cut the heart out of life? For what are we about if not the process? I take my sexual feelings as they come and allow myself to be as I am with them, doing the best I can to separate the past from the present.

*I no longer need to discount myself and others
to fulfill old assumptions that it is not okay to
see clearly and have my power.*

Discounting is a way to drop out and not face
things fully. When my abuse experiences first
came to my memory, I tried lines like, "It wasn't
that bad. . . ." "All parents have power over their
children and it must be almost natural to abuse it
sometimes. . . ." "Who am I to define what they
did as abuse?" I dismissed or trivialized my experience or invalidated my potential to remember
things reliably. These were ways of discounting
myself or the impact of the experience.

In recovery I realize that my power comes
from deep within me. To have this power it is essential that I validate my story to myself and trust
the integrity of my feelings. I begin on a daily basis to take responsibility by doing the opposite of
discounting—letting things count. This includes
considering the feelings of others, which can
make life seem more difficult because I have not
only trivialized my own feelings, but those of
other people at the same time.

Today I will allow myself to grieve for my lost childhood.

I am a child of God and am entitled to live in a safe and protected environment. I deserved to be sheltered and nourished as a child; instead my safety and security were repeatedly under siege and I took cover in whatever ways I could find. Now as I grow more healthy, I am able to release the denial I used to reassure myself that things were not as bad as they seemed. Now I can look back and see that in childhood I was neglected, injured, and never made to feel safe. I lived in an emotional desert. When I see the past clearly, I cannot help feeling heartbreaking sadness for what was missing. But I cannot begin to repair myself further without the willingness to feel it.

Life springs from death. Grief never leaves you where it finds you. My inner child cannot go back and have her childhood over, but she can receive my nurturing today. I can grow more secure with the knowledge that I am learning to seek a safe and protected environment for myself. I can be reassured by knowing I am learning to trust myself by being aware of all my feelings.

I am free to say no to whatever doesn't suit me.
I do not need to take on any guilt or do penance
for saying no.

When I said no as a child, a larger person in authority overrode my protest, even justifying this by telling me it was for my own good. Nowhere in my life was my saying no affirmed. This explains why I grew up unable to say no clearly and simply. When I did say it, it was always laden with guilt and my fear of what my no might mean to someone else.

Today I believe that saying no is an essential way of defining myself and letting my needs and wants be known.

No can be a one-word answer. It does not require elaborate explanation or justification. And when I allow myself to express it free of guilt, the chances are better that it will be received without provoking the person I am refusing. I can say no in any arena of life, including making plans with others, letting a sexual partner know if it is not a good time for me to go on being sexual, and refusing a second date with someone I'd rather not date again. Opportunities present themselves daily for my practice at this form of self-definition.

My search is for the perspective that contains the truth.

As a child I was taught to dismiss my responses and reactions. When I expressed myself directly, I was dismissed in a variety of ways ranging from being ignored to being ridiculed. If I complained about not being heard, I might have been blamed—"You didn't speak up loud enough."

In my healing I seek perspective. I find that I've internalized my parents' dismissal and often dismiss myself even before attempting to be heard. Or I go to an opposite extreme and exaggerate my story, perpetuating the underlying belief that only in their most extravagant form are my thoughts worth hearing.

When I fail to speak up because I fear I will not be heard, I am assuming a personal powerlessness that was the truth of my childhood. Yet it is no longer a place in which I need to be stuck. Today I let my voice out to roam and range fully, seeking the right volume in which to tell my truth.

*I acquire and practice the skills of negotiation,
and learn that compromise can be a satisfying
experience to me.*

As a child who was violated, I became defensive in trying to protect myself. When the needs of others differed from my own, I sensed I was about to lose out and began gathering my armor about me. I felt powerless. I tried to grasp onto anything I could for power, even if I could only have the power of being absent, of withdrawing myself, or the power of being thoroughly hardheaded and sticking to a position even if it made no sense to do so.

I continue to this day to have difficulty negotiating because even hearing the needs of another feels threatening to me when they are different from my own. I respond as if I am about to be violated. I fear stating my own needs clearly because I worry that I will violate another in this same way. But two people cannot begin to negotiate until their individual needs are clearly known and stated. When I make them known and hear another's, I can then participate in creating a solution that can work for both. This experience can be a gift that takes me outside the dynamics of victimization.

*Denial has been a close friend, often protecting
me, yet today I choose to stay aware as I look
on my world.*

If the full breadth of the experience and the
brunt of my feelings about my abuse had to be
known by me all at once, it would have been too
much to bear. Denial has been a curtain for me,
staying closed over selected experiences and feelings. It has protected me and at the same time
kept me in the dark.

Today in my healing I seldom deny my feelings
or my memories. When I hit ruts in my road,
there is a temptation to fall back on denial, but it
is not necessary to do so. If I remind myself I am
in the present, that I have created a safe life for
myself, I can look at my problems and see them
as part of my unfolding. They will not go away
because I cloak them with denial. By staying
aware, I take responsibility for my well-being. I
need not tackle everything at once or find all the
solutions immediately. I can simply be aware of a
problem, sit quietly, and await the acceptance it
requires of me.

*Each day I am presented with an opportunity
to silence myself. Each time I refuse it, I feel
better and grow stronger.*

Every day I get invitations to go back into silence and keep things to myself. The invitations
range from subtle to grand. A subtle one might
be when I have to remind my partner one more
time that I need a certain consideration; a grand
one might be stopping payment on a check because someone has not performed a contracted
service to the agreed-on terms.

Sometimes these invitations come so often I
feel worn down. I yearn for a temporary retire-
ment from life, a vacation from standing up for
myself. Sometimes I even try taking a vacation by
returning to silence, but I find this no longer
works for me. My reservoir for resentments has
shrunken since it has been cleared out, and even
small resentments make me uncomfortable now.
Having experienced some feelings of spaciousness and peace of mind, I miss them very quickly
when they are gone.

I work to break silence each day as the need
arises. At the end of the day, I let go of my actions
and reactions and let myself prepare to be peaceful and present for the next day.

I am empowered by my belief in a higher power who is there to lead me whenever I am ready to surrender.

The exploitation that was exerted over me by my abusers injured me greatly and also distorted my notions of power. As I grew older I wanted only to get further and further from power. I wanted the power to be in charge of myself, to take care of everything alone and have my world under my control, but otherwise I didn't want anything to do with power.

In recovery I've discovered that I need and want to empower myself in many ways. It is not in my higher power's will for me to believe I am unworthy of love, attention, success, admiration, or comfortable economic support. I make a daily practice of telling myself I am worthy and lovable. I realize that when I feel empowered, I am reluctant to let it show because I still hear an old voice telling me that showing my power will lead to further abuse. This voice keeps me away from the universal source of my energy. I turn it off.

Today I have the willingness to accept the love of my higher power and allow it to restore me to my power.

*Today I will allow light to fall on my dark
feelings and show me that I am moving out of
the past.*

As an incest survivor I am easily thrown into
despair, and can feel discouraged by small incidents that do not go my way. But I need only remember that today I can choose to *not* live the
incest experience. It happened in the past and,
while I still need to go through memories, flashbacks, and even reexperiencing some events and
my feelings about them, I choose to take this
journey. I did not choose to participate in the
incest.

Today I can live a wholesome, productive life. I
am fully entitled to give myself all that will please
me: a safe and comfortable home, the love of
friends, a partner if I wish one, and my relationship to my higher power. When I am in pain, I
can let myself know that this too shall pass and
shall come to be meaningful. I can reach out to
others who understand my experience and allow
them to hear me.

By being faithful to myself through both my darkest and lightest hours, I come to know the feeling of an open heart.

As a child it was necessary to abandon my feelings and perceptions to survive. I was not able to directly express the reality of how much I was hurting, whether I held fast to my feelings in some hidden corner of myself or kicked and screamed to act them out.

In my recovery I slowly learn that it is okay to walk through life without faking anything. I often revert to the old tactics—abandoning faithfulness to myself—but as I become more aware, this becomes as painful as my fear of the risks of remaining whole, faithful to myself. Time after time I test the waters, sharing with others who understand my fearfulness. Each time I remain faithful, I feel the regret of the past for how often I was abandoned. I feel the healing of my new commitment. I feel how my faithfulness allows my heart to open and my feet to stand on sturdy ground.

I will wait no longer to enjoy myself but will go ahead and do whatever gives me pleasure today.

Many of us who've been abused have learned to defer our pleasure to some juncture down the road. We may say we want it now but behave as if we do not believe we truly deserve to enjoy ourselves yet. If only our recovery were completed! If only we had finished everything on our superhuman list today! If only someone would tackle us and force us to stop and play now!

The responsibility to enjoy myself is mine alone. So is the privilege. The voices that would have me defer my enjoyment only have as much power as I give them. I have been deluded into believing that enjoyment should be deferred until all else is completed. Using this philosophy, I have often deprived myself. Today the most important thing I can do for my healing may be to take that walk I had thought would be too frivolous, become fully present to play with my children, or do whatever it is that is pleasurable along my path.

*Incorporating my woundedness into my being
makes me whole.*

I look back at childhood pictures and see how
wounded I appear. Yet I still hear the voices of
those who dismissed and shunned me as that
wounded child with statements such as, "Don't
turn your lip out." . . . "Put a smile on your face."
. . . "Crying will get you nowhere." . . . "You've
got nothing to cry about." Much of my life I have
been split off from myself in an effort to avoid
this sad child. But the distance I tried to create
between me and her only became a measure of
my loneliness. For without her I cannot be
whole.

In my healing I have learned that while I regret
that the abuse happened, my pain and suffering
are meaningful. They are the sources that beckon
me to look within, and doing so has given me the
opportunity to deepen myself and seek spiritual
connection. I carry photos of my wounded child
in my wallet and have shown her to others who
were able to see her pain. I do not try to push her
aside, even if her presence might slow me down.
I know I must integrate her, not ignore her, or be
overtaken by her needs. She is part of my being
and recognizing that makes me whole.

The longer I remain abstinent and in active recovery from my addictions, the more I give myself a chance to grow and develop enough to face my abuse.

Many of us abuse survivors fell prey to alcohol and other drug addiction, or other compulsive behaviors, such as under- or overeating, co-dependency, sexual compulsiveness, or compulsive spending or gambling. At first my compulsive behaviors and addiction were useful for medicating me, holding me apart from the pain of my experiences. But eventually the addiction ceased working in any sort of life-enhancing way and became another source of victimization and loss of control, robbing me of connection with my true self.

In recovery from addiction I seek the support of others who are also getting well. I focus first on developing a strong base for my sobriety or abstinence and then take the time to celebrate the achievement of putting down the drug or behavior I abused. I need not plunge headlong into examining all my incest issues; instead I allow them to be set aside until I am ready. When I am ready, the model of my recovery from addiction can provide hope for me and serve as a blueprint for dealing with my incest.

*I know and use tools to move away from stress
rather than perpetuate it.*

No one can avoid stress, yet we can help ourselves out of it by not getting stuck going round
and round inside it and feeling victimized by being stuck. As abuse survivors, we may even be
addicted to the adrenaline high of a crisis, to protecting our anger, and to the wariness that comes
as a natural response when we feel threatened.

But we rarely experience deep pleasure while
in a stressed condition. We deserve a release from
the rush of adrenaline and the imperative for self-
protection.

I counter stress from various approaches. I talk
out what is provoking me with a friend. I do yoga
or some other exercise that takes me temporarily
outside of my problem and gives my body another focus. I take a few quiet moments to make
contact with my higher power and open myself
to the flow of this wisdom. When I return to the
stressful problem, it will still be there but my
ability to work with it will be altered.

Energy is the flow of life within me; I envision letting it run like a river.

Too much effort blocks the flow of life in us, and yet how can we direct ourselves toward healing without exerting it? I begin with the intention to sift through past abuse and "deal" with it. But what do I mean by this? Do I go into thrashing battle with my memories, seeking to exorcise them or purge myself all at once of the ways they've affected me? Do I feel more frustrated than ever that I have not reached a final resting place?

I stop to consider whether I am wearing myself out by fighting resistance that arises in me when my effort is too great. I aim my effort at becoming willing to explore, and recognize that true liveliness is in the process of exploring.

I do not need to finish anything today. I only need to be wholly in the moment, to see what is before me, and to be open to the flow of my energy. Whatever lies before me is not blocking my next step; it *is* my next step.

I am entitled to be whole in mind, body, and spirit. Today I will practice holding these spheres in balance.

I have a natural desire for harmony, for achieving a state of balance in which all aspects of myself are given respect and attention. In my family of origin, it was frequently impossible to remain harmonious. I sometimes needed to leave my body for self-preservation. I glommed onto the intellectual sphere to try to make sense of things. And I grasped at any spiritual sign as a way to sail far away from my problems. But this left me out of balance, tossing in the waves, missing my ground, feeling unrooted.

Today I allow the Serenity Prayer to guide me:

God grant me the serenity
To accept the things I cannot change,
The courage to change the things I can,
And the wisdom to know the difference.

I cannot change my family or my past; I cannot live it any differently than I lived it. But I can today make the decision to consciously choose a balanced life. I can add more of whatever ingredients are missing. I can correct as soon as I notice I am out of balance. I do not need to wait for a difficult and painful crisis before I make my adjustments. In this way, with the help of my higher power, I will create a life that suits me and keeps me healthy.

*I allow myself to cry freely and let out my deep
sadness.*

I was discouraged from crying as a child. The
expression of my feelings threatened others and I
was told, "It won't get you anywhere to cry, so
stop it." No one held me. No one seemed to understand that crying unhindered for a while
would be self-limiting and come to an end. I perceived the discomfort of others and tried in every
way possible to stop myself from crying to com-
ply with their needs.

Today when I return with my inner child to
the memories of my childhood, I can give myself
the gift of a full cry. I feel the brokenheartedness
in the center of my chest. I howl like a wolf cub
abandoned by its mother. I defy the voices of my
childhood if they speak up to tell me to stop crying. I stay with the desire to fully express this sorrow. I trust it to bend of its own accord when I
am finished. I allow my tears to be witnessed,
and if I want I can ask someone unafraid of my
tears to comfort me.

I know that when the sadness passes, my heart
will open.

*Through daily meditation I remember to trust
in the greater direction of my higher power.*

Because I was unable to control my destiny as a
child, I cling fiercely now to the need to exert my
will as if that is the highest source of power. Yet I
have come to believe in the existence of a force I
call a higher power. It is a relief to hand my will
over to this power. And whenever I do so I am
convinced that the fierce clinging never lent me
any real power at all—only the illusion of power.

When I trust in the greater direction of my
higher power, more possibilities are opened up to
me than I could ever have imagined. Even when
I feel as if I am not being given what I need, I
have a basic sense of well-being I never had without my faith.

Because I am quick to forget my faith and revert to old ways, I make a practice of daily meditation. In this way I jog the memory of the new
me, the believer, and gain a good orientation for
my day.

I recognize that holding on to unrealistic expectations leads to disappointment, so I try my best to let them go as I become aware of them.

When I am full of unrealistic expectations, I am bound to become disappointed and unreasonable, for I have predicted a future without considering the needs of others. It is humbling to realize how often I make this error. Why do I do it over and over?

As an incest survivor, I tried desperately to grasp at whatever I thought might give me some control. I liked school because the questions seemed to have answers. If I studied carefully, I could predict getting the right answers on the quiz. I felt comforted in an environment where things were predictable and not so arbitrary. But in many areas of life, things are not predictable. I do better to accept this uncertainty than if I expect an outcome based on my own wishes. Even with myself, I deprive myself of spontaneity when I believe I know exactly what to expect.

I will live in the day and stop concerning myself with what may happen next. I will be pleasantly surprised as I relax my expectations of this moment. Many of my burdens will fall away, and I will have fewer problems than I thought I had.

I humbly recognize my right relationship to this earth, other beings, and my creator.

The root of the word *humility* is the same as that of *humus*, which means earth. To be humble is to walk with my feet firmly on the ground, knowing I have been given a place and time to be on this planet. I need not puff up with arrogance, fly away with grandiosity, or pride myself on being perfect to be noticed or feel accounted for.

In the abusive situation of my childhood, I was thrown off center and needed to shield myself with one of many personas to allay my extreme vulnerability. My self had to shrink to survive the humiliation of the abuse. Consequently, I needed to create a grandiose outer self to compensate for my inner shrunken self so that I could feel capable of being out in the world.

Now I fear that to humble myself will be humiliating—that it will be a reminder of that inner shrunken self of the past. But by taking the risk I discover this is not so. When I stop trying to make things go my way and turn the reins over to my higher power, I am relieved of a great burden and become exactly the right size, neither too large nor too small, simply me.

*I affirm my desire to do meaningful work and
my ability to perform it in a vitalizing way.*

Meaningful work can nurture me. It is within
my power to orient my life so that I do not feel
victimized by my work but energized by it. If I
have fallen into a trap of doing work that does
not satisfy me in any way and only drains me,
part of my recovery may be to find a way to
change this.

Even when we are not aware of it, we often
choose a particular profession or trade for a reason. For instance, those of us who chose to work
in the health professions may have unconsciously
become healers out of a desire to heal ourselves.
This was a positive use of the empathy we derived from our own injuries. But, as we do more
direct healing, we may find ourselves ambivalent
about going on with our job. Sometimes we jump
to the conclusion that we must change our job
when we only need to change our attitude.

Therefore, before I make major changes, I will
seek to see my work in a new light. If I have been
working compulsively, I will look for ways to
achieve balance. If I have problems with people I
work with, I will take them one at a time and determine what I can change.

I accept fatigue as an okay condition of my body and spirit. It instructs me in my limits.

It seemed particularly dangerous to be tired in my childhood, perhaps because I feared being more greatly injured if I put my armor down. Or because I did not dare relax for fear of being overwhelmed by my feelings. I may have been so far removed from my body that I did not receive its signals of fatigue.

In my recovery I learn to be pleased by being present in my body. This allows me both pleasure and pain, and I come to know various levels of tiredness. I become acquainted with these levels like floors in a building. I can get off and rest at the top floor, the first sign of fatigue, or I can ignore it and get off on lower floors. If I get off lower, though, the process of restoring myself will be longer and slower. Sometimes, even knowing it will be more painful to go lower, I still have to do that, for I make progress but I do not always awaken as fast as I would like to. I am grateful to be able to live in and with my body and learn to trust it.

Today I will acknowledge the strides I have taken in recovery.

Because I am recovering, I can begin to interpret my past differently. I can look back and, rather than be discouraged by the reality of the injuries, I can be encouraged by how much my perspective has changed. I notice I feel less shame because I have ceased to believe the myth that I was somehow responsible for the abuse. I notice I am no longer willing to take responsibility for anyone but myself. I hold others accountable for their behavior; I do not need to figure them out or understand them.

While my incest memories remain painful, I do not regret looking at them and working to remember my past experiences, for in doing so I am reclaiming my power that was lost to them. I am growing by regaining my experience. Acquiring and integrating my experience makes my life more real and full, and makes my behaviors and feelings in the past comprehensible.

*I open my heart and let love flow in and out
of it.*

Abuses in my childhood closed my heart like a
fist. Living this way deprives me of joy, of the
flow of love. I clutch at survival. I wish to find
safety. I beat everyone back and let my fortress be
seen, but inside I am forlorn, neglected, and
alone.

I can reverse this not by building on to my im-
penetrable fortress but by becoming willing to
open a door. I tune into the hardness of the fist of
my heart and realize I am clinging to fear. I cannot change the past, but I can change my relationship to this fear. I breathe in and out of it and
notice how reliable my breathing is—a life force
like my heartbeat.

I recognize and speak to the fear. I do not wish
to ignore it. I tell it I understand where it came
from and why I have needed it. I tell it I will not
forget what created it, but I would also like release from it now to try other ways. I breathe long
and slow and gradually feel the fear dissolve. I
feel untried and uncertain without it, but if I ven-
ture out a little and let my love flow I will gain a
new experience.

I was taught to fear my anger, but I can learn to use it wisely to protect myself.

Anger was not legitimized in my childhood. It was expressed as the tyrant's tirade, by my father only. I learned that anger could be used to control and intimidate those with less power. When anger rose up in me, I wanted only to get away from it. I was uncomfortable in my own skin. I did not want anger to make me into a tyrant, but I had been shown no other use for it.

As I heal I become aware that when I feel squirrelly I need to check out my anger and become conscious of it, lest I become self-abusive, put myself down, or become ill. I learn to let myself feel it, even prize it for its protective quality. If my anger says, "Step back, take some distance, open your eyes wide," I abide it. Next I look for constructive ways to express my anger. I may need to find a safe place to scream or beat pillows, alone or witnessed by my therapist. I may need to confront someone. Again, I create a safe situation in which to do this. For instance, in the separation of a relationship I may need the help of a lawyer or mediator. I can be fueled by my anger and yet act wisely.

*Only by reaching out for the help I need will I
be able to take care of myself fully.*

I am accustomed to going it alone. Those I
needed for basic support and validation abused
me or stood by and failed to protect me. Therefore I believed I could only be safe if I were completely independent and able to take care of my
own needs. I imagined that I would be safe and
well when I could accomplish this.

In the healing process I learn that we are all
meant to rely on each other. I do not need to become a plumber, an auto mechanic, a doctor, and
a lawyer to be safe in the world; I do not have to
know how to do everything by myself. I realize
now that when I make a decision without review-
ing my problem with anyone, I do not have a full
perspective. Sharing my feelings allows me to become unencumbered. To try to do it all alone is
not the solution to my fear of trusting, which
came from the abuse. Others who I can trust are
on my path today. Gradually I begin to reach out
by making phone calls, sharing my problems,
and asking for the help I need. When others
reach back, it sustains me, opens my mind beyond its restrictions, and lets me know I am
loved.

I respect my inner guide and the strength this source has always provided me to survive and move toward healing.

My spirit has not been easy to sustain. It is important to acknowledge this but to realize as well that I have developed certain strengths because of it.

I've long had an inner guide who kept me going and created safe spaces where I could reside in some peace. My guide directed me to the outdoors where I took solace in nature. She guided me to fantasies of a warm, nurtured life that provided the possibility of well-being. She guided me to draw forth a well of patience when to react more rebelliously would have caused greater injury.

Some of these strengths I now discover woven through the old patterns and character defects that I would like to leave behind. But even as I prepare to part with old ways, it is important to look back with honor and compassion on the strengths that brought me this far, and to distinguish the warp from the woof. For instance, I can learn to live in reality without giving up my imagination. And I can retain the quality of patience without misusing it to outlast someone else in righteous indignation.

*I thank the Great Mother Earth for providing
me firm ground to stand on and struggle from.*

Of the four elements—fire, air, water, earth—
earth is the one I have always been aware of carrying me through distressed times. In the beauty
of her forms and colors, I sought and received solace as a child. When there was total distress in
my house, I went outside, smelled the earth,
walked or ran on the ground, and gradually received some of her solidity.

As I heal I become more consciously aware of
her gifts to me. She gives me gravity through
which I can feel my body in relation to her. This
relationship is steady and consistent, unlike how
I felt about my body when I was being abused
and needed to let parts of me fly away. Now I feel
my feet coming to stand more sturdily on the
ground. I do not let anyone push me around. If I
feel crowded I take a good stance and make a little elbow room.

I respect this Great Mother as both source and
inspiration for my growing.

Today I focus on my healing.

We work hard to uncover memories, to let the raw material creep out of the closed trunks it had been stored in. We are horrified and then weep and grieve at the experiences we encountered, and our powerlessness over them. But is this healing? We become disoriented and more frightened than ever because we have let things out but do not yet have a perspective. It is easy in this condition for us to feel more wounded than ever.

The recalling, the exposing, the revealing to myself and others is all part of my healing. But I need a more conscious sense of salving my wounds too. I seek those ways that are right for my nature. I might cleanse myself with ritual. I might sit at the ocean and give my sorrow to the Great Mother and receive new energy with each wave that comes in. I might say "I love you" to myself many times a day.

I do not need anyone's permission to heal from my abusive childhood, but I do seek the encouragement and help of others.

I commit myself to being honest with myself and others today.

I deserve honesty as my way of life today and every day. In the past I did not feel safe enough to tell things as they were or even to see things as they were. This deprived me of closeness with myself. I needed to cover for others to protect them. I no longer need to do that. In fact, my growth is in direct proportion to how honest I am. My first responsibility is to speak up about my needs and feelings, even when I fear that doing so will affect others. I will not be oblivious to how I affect others, but neither will I try to alter myself by anticipating their responses.

When I make my feelings secret, the one I hurt first and most is me. For how can I see clearly while hiding certain aspects of myself? Remaining as true as possible to myself each day builds my self-esteem and lets me feel right with myself.

April

*A glimpse of grace is worth all my hard work
and pain. It heartens me to know another is at
hand though I have no formula to produce it.*

What is grace? A moment of wholeness?
The alignment of my life with the purpose of the
universe?

Despite the pain of an abusive childhood, we
can each remember moments of grace throughout it—the sensation of sun on our hair in a
meadow, our trusting dog licking our face, the
still magic of holding a new baby. These moments go on into adult life. They were fewer during the years of duress when we paid little
attention to our ·spiritual connection. Yet perhaps they were lights all strung together that kept
us going.

Today I am blessed with the awareness that
grace is always nearby, yet not in the least a quality that responds to manipulation. I am relieved
by this notion. It frees me from drive and tells me
that I receive grace when I am open and receptive
and willing. It is nothing I need to try for. It is
something to be appreciated and enjoyed.

I am a whole person and have the potential to bring together all the different aspects of myself.

A fairly common defense incest victims use during the experience is to split off, to go out of body and into an observer's role. This split can be the beginning of a split in which we have more than one picture of ourselves. We might be an overachieving "good" girl in one picture, a whore in another, a tough, unreachable rebel in yet another.

I sometimes continue to see myself in split ways; it causes me trouble and contributes to a lack of satisfaction with myself. For I do not feel whole as long as I am housed in one persona and then another. I give out conflicting messages to myself and others. I deserve the integration of these personas.

Working to know myself better will help me heal on this journey. So will understanding that whenever I see only black-or-white choices, I need to wait longer before making a decision. The black-and-white choices only satisfy one persona or another, not the full me.

*When fear holds me captive, I will turn outside
myself to find a helping hand.*

Fear drives obsession and can keep me going
round and round the same track until I drop
from exhaustion. But I can learn tools to inter-
rupt that cycle.

In my abusive family I did not find a safe place
to turn. When I tried to reach for help by crying,
I encountered further abuse, ridicule, or humiliation for exhibiting "weakness." I built armor
around my fear and pain; I didn't share it and feel
it be lifted. There were exceptions to this: some
people in my life did hold out a hand and sometimes the notion of a higher power touched and
consoled me.

In recovery I have a chance to deal much more
consciously with my fear. I share it with others. I
distinguish the present from the past. I love and
cherish my wounded inner child. I admit when
fear makes my life unmanageable. I allow myself
to accept where I am on my journey. I allow myself to accept that I am fearful, and at the same
time know that I am going to be all right.

I will give the respect I want to myself and others.

A key element of respect is allowing each person, including myself, to be whole. This runs contrary to the distorted notions of respect I picked up through my abuse experiences. In my childhood I was not respected. I was taught to accommodate a double standard that mandated I respect my elders though they were not required to respect their children.

I struggle in recovery to learn how to respect myself a day at a time. I am surprised when I take a close look to discover that not only do I often fail to demand respect for myself, I fail to truly respect others. I have been deeply trained to ignore the needs of others when they conflict with my own. Reacting immediately to defend myself or trying to talk the other person out of his or her need does not show respect for the other person's wholeness. If I turn inward, I recognize my actions come from my fear that I will not be able to take care of myself. I show respect for myself by hearing myself out. I consciously turn off the old messages and also hear others out.

I open my eyes to see the gifts of recovery I am receiving.

To do our healing we must creep through some pretty dark tunnels. To re-member ourselves in the painful times of the past is not easy and often leaves us battle-scarred and exhausted. It is important from time to time to cast our vision more consciously onto the fruits of our recovery so that we may see our efforts are well worthwhile.

In denial I was flat, apathetic, often bored, perhaps depressed. In recovery I am energized and my life seems full of feeling, even if the predominant feeling is sometimes rage. Before recovery I was always plagued with the underlying feeling that no matter what happened, I would end up the victim. Now I know a much different experience in which I see that life makes its offerings to me—good news and bad news even in the same day. I am there to relate to it, not to be defined by it or made its victim.

I will take the time to focus on my purpose and realize my path is being guided by my higher power.

We each have a purpose. Mine may sometimes feel elusive but that is not because it has disappeared; it is because I have lost awareness of it. My purpose is guided by a design of which I can see only segments at any one time. I trust I am exactly where I am supposed to be, and I do not need to do anything but wait if I cannot see an open door before me.

One of my jobs as an incest survivor is to regain my personal power. My relationship to power was distorted by the perpetrator's abuse of it. When I am living in my past, I become powerless again. I feel weak, prone to victimization, and crumble easily at the thought of needing to take action. But in the present I can learn to come into my power. It is not a power *over*, in which someone else must be oppressed. It is the power of *being present* in a relationship of oneness with the universe. It is the power of my faith in the notion that if I seek guidance, I will intuitively know the next right thing to do. It is the power of deeply knowing my spirit is fully entitled to the life I have been given. I do not need to barter for this power by giving up parts of myself.

I will order my day according to what is important to me.

Unless I am selective, there is often more to do than I can fit into twenty-four hours with ease. A measure of my maturity is my growing ability to make choices and live with the consequences of them. Then I do not become a victim of my sacrifices.

The concept of sacrificing some things to narrow my options to suit my priorities is especially frightening to me as an incest survivor, because as a child I felt I was the sacrifice. The sanctity of my being was violated. This made me confused about setting priorities and kept me clinging to a belief that safety lay in nothing being left out or discarded.

In recovery I realize overextending myself with activities or people can leave me without enough time to nurture and attend to myself. I cannot give with true generosity if I have shortchanged myself. Today I practice taking full responsibility for choosing what I want and need, and in what order. I will allow myself to feel fully satisfied with my choices.

*Ordering my life according to my priorities and
bringing projects to completion gives me a
sense of validity and substance.*

As a child under siege by abuse, my life was
chaotic and reactive, moving as if according to
which way the wind was blowing. Little was predictable or reliable. I sought to find order in a
family that masked its dysfunction with disorder.

As I begin to heal, I yearn for a life in which I
can rest peacefully and feel the achievement that
comes with completing projects. Instead of creating crises as my mode for action, I see that it is
possible to put myself on a course and follow it to
satisfaction. I may feel anxious about finishing
things, about reaching the moment where it becomes apparent that I have left behind my family's way of jumping from one crisis to another.
But I remain steadfast and seek the guidance of
my higher power to stabilize me like a rudder
that will help me stay on course.

I allow myself to develop and learn to use judgment while refraining from judging others unfairly.

I am learning to trust, based on my using good judgment. I need to experiment to know if I am in a safe situation. Then I can make accurate judgments about the effects other people, places, or things will have on me in the situations I choose to enter.

I can learn to use my judgment for my own protection. My ability to respond to my gut instincts was closed down years ago in response to the abuse; I was not able to protect myself. Now I choose to learn how to protect myself.

As I develop my ability to make judgments I can trust, I need to be alert to when and how I judge others. In the past, I judged others as an act of self-defense. I used my judging to trump up self-righteous justification of my feelings. Today I know it is okay for me to have my feelings, simply because they are part of my being. I do not need to justify them by judging others. Others' motives can never be fully known by me. I am free to let go and be human and let others be human too.

I release the impulse to hoard that grew from deprivation and experience the renewal that comes of sharing generously.

Those of us whose needs went unmet in childhood may have turned to hoarding as a way to try to accumulate "enough" of anything. Or we may have developed habits of keeping accomplishments or compliments to ourselves, even hiding them so they wouldn't be vulnerable to the scrutiny of others. Consequently, we may have repressed our talents rather than having developed and shared them.

In recovery we learn that our healing is best reinforced by sharing. We keep mindful of where we have been and what we have learned by being available to help others who are on a similar journey.

As I listen to someone just beginning to deal with incest, I remember the pain and disorientation of first opening myself up to this exploration. As I share my progress, I document my movement. As I share my hope, it is doubled. I demonstrate my belief in the statement: If any one of us can recover, then we all can.

I heal both by reparenting my inner child and by parenting my children in a loving, responsible fashion.

My parenting skills require a lot of work and conscious development, for I do not want to fall back on the example I learned from my own protectors who abused me. I sense that they too had been abused as children and were compelled to act out of their own pain. We may be doomed to repeat our past unless we become conscious of it. I have the good fortune of coming of age when the opportunity to identify what happened to me is possible.

If I am still acting like my own parents and not giving love freely to myself, I may feel jealous of the love I want to give my children. I can right that by paying attention to my own needs. When I am loved, I am able to give love. When I am needy, I can go to appropriate sources to receive nurturing. My children are not appropriate sources. It is my job to nurture them, not their job to nurture me.

Developing and communicating my boundaries is important for both me and my children. It shows my children an example of someone who is fallible but accountable.

I choose to live with the positive attitudes of hope and renewal that are generated by spring.

When we have lived through a long winter, we are rejuvenated by spring. Our desire for longer and stronger light is satisfied by the sun and we sit outside or in a window and drink in its healing powers. Crocuses come up and remind us of how colorful all gardens will soon be. Watching the new growth, more seems possible.

I have lived too long surrounded with the darkness from my early life. No matter how far along I am in my recovery, because I am on the journey I can see light and reach toward it. I can choose today to live with positive attitudes. There will always be some things going in my favor and some that feel as if they are bringing me down. In the familiar victim role, I will be more comfortable choosing to concentrate on the negative. But if I concentrate on the positive, I will experience the power of renewal and know spring.

I will live my life in the present, in the way it has been given, in the day, in the moment.

I have a day before me. I will live it today as best I can. I will cease acting as if I were in dress rehearsal for my real life, which has always seemed a step away from where I was. That notion has deprived me.

In the traumatic times of my childhood, I survived by leaving the present, by literally believing, "It can't be me this is happening to." To escape the moment, I projected myself into the future or reached back to cling to some moment or myth from the past.

Today I want the fullness of the day as it is presented to me. This means walking through painful moments, feeling joy, and allowing myself other emotions like affection and fear that in the past seemed incompatible in the same moment. Allowing myself this range of emotions may be frightening to my inner child, who took refuge by exiting the present. But if I am truly present now, I can give her reassurance as part of living on my own terms.

My fear of being loved is an outgrowth of my past; I will no longer permit it to drive me away from natural fulfillment.

When I was a child, one of the people I depended on for love misused my trust and dependency by abusing me. While I intuitively knew there was something wrong with that, I was too young and powerless to throw off its influence. So I translated it into these lessons: love comes hand in hand with abuse; I must deserve no better; and I can't have one without the other.

Today this is no longer okay with me. As I heal I want to love and be loved free of abuse. When love flows smoothly in a relationship, I sometimes feel it is too good to be true and become eager to find a glitch to sabotage the relationship. Or if I have chosen a partner who is equally nervous and new at this, she or he will do this for me.

The solution is not in analysis but in allowing myself to be in love—to realize love as a life force given by my higher power. The abuser distorted it but never had the power to take it from me. It simply lies dormant waiting for the healed me to express it.

*By attending to my inner child, I find the space
I need in which to grow up and become
responsible for myself.*

With a background of abuse, it is easy to get
stuck in my childhood, circling round and round
with my unmet needs, moving toward them,
then away, not truly willing to commit to taking
care of them for fear if I take this job seriously, I
will be letting my abusers off the hook. But the
only one I hurt in thinking this way is myself.

It is natural for my inner child to want to seek
reparations, to believe it is not too late to receive
what I failed to receive from a parent or close rel-
ative. In some cases, it may be possible through
confrontation to receive money for therapy or
some other compensation. But compensation
alone will not heal my wounds.

When I stop shunning my inner child and decide to become her trustworthy protector, I begin
to understand what it means to be responsible. I
am no longer dependent on others to take care of
me. I can recognize and build confidence in the
life skills and experience I have acquired and put
them to very good use by being present to reassure my inner child.

I am learning to take my power without fearing that I am taking power away from someone else.

I am beginning to sense how power was taken away from me as a child. I was not seen, not heard, not encouraged to develop my own voice and talents. Today in recovery I wish to take my power, not to abuse or take anything away from another, but to be in harmony with and act for myself. Each time I say no to something I do not want, I am exerting my power to establish my boundaries. Each time I act to reinforce these boundaries, I grow stronger, less like a victim.

I have learned first what I do not want; it is more difficult still to say what I do want and to assert myself in that way. I recognize that this is a part of my development that did not happen in childhood. It will now come awkwardly, until I am able to season it with experience.

One thing I want is a peaceful heart and mind. I seek this a day at a time through conscious contact with the Goddess of my understanding, and by keeping myself on the journey of learning who I am and how I can set myself straight with the world. This does not mean I will not continue to make mistakes, but that I understand now how to own them and make amends for my errors as close as possible to the time they were made.

My intuition guides me; I learn to trust its integrity.

My intuition comes from a deep inner source and gives me a reading on my soul. Yet so much interference runs like static between it and the part of me that is trying to make decisions that I am often unable to trust it with any certainty.

During the abuse I had an intuitive sense that I was being mistreated, even though the perpetrator told me that what was being done was for my own good, that I was being "loved" or attended to, and that I had better shut up about it. I had to twist my intuitive information by discounting it. This left me without protection against potential invasions and molestations, for even when I could feel inside that something was off, I still couldn't say no.

In my healing I learn to trust in the integrity of my intuition. I still encounter confusion. I do not always know immediately what my intuitive response means, but I practice taking it into account and holding it in my perceptions with high value. If I sit quietly with it, eventually the air will clear and I will be able to let my intuition guide me.

I tap the power of ritual as a healing tool for separating my present from my past.

Sexual abuse has had a profound impact on the way we have carried ourselves into adult life. Even if we thought we had managed to ignore its influence for years, the painful reality will be evident when we begin to open the places where we have buried our feelings, where we have split off from the wounded part of ourselves. Then we can see all the opportunities we have passed by, the avenues we have avoided as if they were cordoned off by police barriers.

I need ways to declare myself a new, wholly present person, no longer the victim of vagueness, no longer the invisible lost soul. Designing personal rituals is one way to help me connect with the present. I can call up the power of ritual with a simple act like lighting a candle or burning incense. I can attach to this act a symbolic significance such as bringing light into my heart or healing through the odor of a certain incense I burn. I can then affirm who I am today and separate from my past, letting it exist as it truly was but releasing myself from its influence on me.

Letting go is a never-ending process of relating to my resistance.

When I let go of my nearly unrelenting need to control, my belief that I can bend even iron with my will, I am released into serenity and trust in a power greater than myself. Then, almost immediately, I drop the most powerful lesson I have learned and take up my willfulness again. I ask myself in some bewilderment, why would I do this?

To some extent, my need for control may have become excessive and obsessive because the loss of control in the sexual abuse was so great that I needed to make up for it. But regardless of my history, it is also a very human characteristic to grasp for control. The way to work with this is through a daily practice of noticing what I am clinging to—a thought, a feeling, a memory, a determination to make a situation come out a certain way—and uncurling my grip as a gesture of release and watching what I am clinging to float away. Releasing my willful attachments creates space and sustenance for my soul.

Today I recognize my capacity to mature, live my own life, and know what I want, directing myself to it in an effective manner.

I was thrust into what felt like an adult role early in childhood, but I received little actual orientation about how to grow up or how to take care of myself properly. I resent the role I was forced to play—emotional confidant and "lover" to a parent. I resent the way my childhood was robbed of its ease and innocence.

Holding on to these resentments does not punish the perpetrators. It punishes me. I need to remember the things that happened to me in the past and realize their impact on me, but I do not need to cling to the resentments. Today I can allow myself to grow into a mature adult who is capable of tending to my inner child, and who also can bring my presence fully into the world. One day at a time I will learn what I want and how to direct myself to move effectively toward it. I will begin to integrate envisioning what I want with doing the footwork necessary to achieve it. I will trust that my higher power is a constant in guiding me.

*I respect my desires and put forth my wants
and needs, asking others to meet them, despite
the risk that they might not be able to.*

In the past I learned to put aside my desires so
habitually that I now have to make a conscious
effort to even know what they are. Knowing what
they are is the first step in the process of finding
the resources to meet them. Becoming aware of
them can make me uncomfortable. It can raise
the spectre of old feelings of deprivation, of the
trauma I experienced when my desires were not
treated respectfully. Reaching for my desires is a
way of claiming my right to life and contradicts
the way I long ago convinced myself it was better
to recede into a small space and ask for nearly
nothing.

In my recovery a steady stream of opportunities presents itself for me to stand fast with my
wants and needs. I sometimes dread these occa-
sions and wish they would be saved for another
day, but I trust my higher power knows what I
can handle. I try to use each situation as a chance
to see my new strength, to feel the legitimacy of
my desires and needs, and to leave behind the
old system of denying their existence, which did
not allow me to take care of myself.

Each time I let go of a secret, I grow into myself more soundly.

Secrets keep us in an awkward balance, tiptoeing around when we want to be standing firmly on the ground. Many of us when abused in childhood were threatened with severe consequences for telling. In other cases our instructions to keep quiet were more subtle—we were raised to protect Mom or Dad from the consequences of their actions. We were seduced into believing that they could be there for us if only we would protect them by our silence.

In recovery I learn that each secret I keep closes a door to my heart. I begin one by one to disclose these secrets, first by sharing them with other survivors and my therapist. In my relationships, I practice telling the truth. I do not need to hide my feelings. Each time I find myself concealing what I feel in order to protect the other person, I do my best to reveal myself honestly. No longer is a relationship based on my improperly protecting another person worth my while. When I am ready I can also disclose my memories and feelings to my perpetrator, if I want to choose this avenue.

Today I will let loneliness lead me closer to myself.

When I was abused as a child, I moved away from myself. I turned off completely from feeling my body. I spaced out and went into secret pockets of my imagination. This gave me a way to protect myself, but it also made me feel extremely isolated and lonely.

Today I sometimes feel lonely while alone, in a crowded room, or even with a friend or partner. It is my inner state that makes me feel this way—an emptiness or longing for something I do not have. If I focus on the emptiness, it may begin to fill with feelings I would rather avoid, such as abandonment, anger, or grief. If I stop trying to control these feelings, surrender to feeling them, and stay present in the moment, I connect with me and the loneliness passes. I may also need to share these feelings with a friend or with my incest survivors group. To have my experience witnessed lets me see myself more clearly.

I am a fully entitled citizen of the world and do not need to justify the path I am walking.

Because my early relationship to myself as a separate growing person was damaged by the abuse, I did not develop the belief that I was meant to be. I had an intuitive sense that this was so, yet no one in my family validated it. Thus, my intuitive feeling provoked the ambivalent answer: maybe, maybe not. Thus, I became prone to justifying my existence and my actions to try to escape this conflict.

Today I do not need to justify who I am, where I am, or why I am there. I am moving along my journey and only a power greater than myself can see the larger picture of my life. As long as I am willing to be honest and am following out the steps that are laid before me to the best of my ability, I do not need to concern myself with what others think of me. If others challenge me, I do not need to justify myself. I can keep in mind that just as I do not know enough about any other human being to judge their motivations, neither is it right for anyone else to judge mine.

I make a continual practice of self-love, whether I am up or down, sick or well, tired or well-rested.

There may be nothing harder than sticking to a policy of self-love regardless of the flux of my feelings. For when things are not going the way I want them to, when my expectations are not being fulfilled, I immediately begin the old pattern of shoveling myself into the garbage as if I am a useless failure.

If I stop and take note when I take out the shovel, I will be able to realize that as a child I had few resources to keep alive the sense of myself as lovable. But now I am free to develop all the resources I need. I have friends to call who will remind me I am loved. I can look at my face in the mirror and affirm my love for myself. I can hug myself or my teddy bear and console the child within me. I can slow down and become aware of my higher power as a force that I can trust to lead me and provide for me all that I need, even when I am unable to see the provisions.

I take a step back to think, rather than acting impulsively on my pride.

My pride is a function of my ego. Sometimes I want to be right so badly that I am willing to be dishonest and exert myself strongly in error rather than say a simple, "I don't know," or "I think I was wrong there." This only causes problems in my relations with other people and in my relationship to myself. Yet looking back on my childhood, I can see why I would do it. For others exerted their rightness over me with authority, not honesty. And I perceived that as the usual position of power.

In my healing I seek my power and realize it does not come in this way. My pride does not need to have the first and last word. I can take the time to think things through and feel my feelings. Then my pride will sit back and allow my true power to emerge.

I realize courage is available to everyone, including me.

In the past I took my fearfulness to mean I lacked courage. I imagined courageous people were those who were fearless. But now I know that in my survival from the incest I have displayed the courage to keep myself going through despair—through circumstances deeply destructive to my self-esteem. Like a weed growing out of a crack in a rock, I clung tenaciously to life and survived until I was ready for healing.

In recovery my fears feel accentuated as I become more conscious of them. I realize my powerlessness acutely as I stand on a precipice where I cannot go back to the old way but neither can I clearly see the way forward. I sometimes mistake this powerlessness for a lack of courage. But this is when I need to take a deep breath and allow myself a quiet moment to ask for the help of my higher power. And realizing that there may be great satisfaction in the experience that frightens me, I step willingly into it. Courage is with me like a friend.

I am learning to recognize flashbacks for what they are so I can work with them rather than let them stop me in my tracks.

Many times I have been totally thrown by a flashback without even knowing I was having one. If I suddenly feel small and inadequate for what I am about to face, I am probably in a flashback. Sometimes I have run away from the task at hand because I was eager to escape those vulnerable feelings. Sometimes I have become inappropriately tough, angry, arrogant, or demanding to mask my smallness and helplessness.

Flashbacks often come when I seek to take my power. I step forth to give a lecture. I make a commitment to a relationship that is good for me. I want to perform well at a job interview. I know I have the capabilities required and can be well prepared. Yet when the moment comes to carry myself forward, I do so haltingly, as if I am a nearly invisible child. Rather than experience this pain, I have often dropped out of activities that would have given me satisfaction.

As I learn to recognize a flashback for what it is, I can walk through the painful feelings with the help of my fellow survivors and my higher power and stop narrowing my world out of avoidance.

I will love my inner child unconditionally.

To heal from the abuse I suffered, it is important to develop a loving relationship with my inner child. This may take time but begins when I am willing to visualize and talk with her. In my first glimpses it may seem threatening to see her, for she brings memories of deep feeling. She may seem pathetic and ugly, weak and unbearably vulnerable. She may be a ball of rage and want nothing to do with me. Whatever I visualize, I must first accept her exactly as she is and cease to wish she would be otherwise. This acceptance in itself is love and she will know she can trust it.

Once our relationship has begun, I will nurture it by talking to my inner child often. I will ask her to tell me what she wants and needs from me. I will hold her and stroke her and examine just how hurt she is. I will ask her to talk back to me and let me know how best I can help her heal. I will reassure her that I will use the growing strengths of my recovery to protect her and nurture her. I am not acquiring them so I can pretend she is a drag on me and run from her. I want to and will love her unconditionally.

As my memory grows fuller, I feel more whole and know myself more deeply.

My memory protects me by blocking out certain painful events in my life, holding them in an unconscious storehouse until I grow strong enough to add them to the picture. I am only able to fill out the picture by placing myself in supportive situations, such as in therapy and in sharing with groups of others who understand my experience. My memories are jarred by such sharing, as is my awareness of the gaps in my memory.

When I remember the abuse experiences, I sometimes first remember the incidents without the feelings attached to them. Other times I remember the feelings without being able to recall the specifics. I dread receiving the memories because of the painful, powerless feelings attached to them. But each time I experience a new memory, a spacious feeling grows inside me and restores the balance of my spirit. I know myself more deeply. The ways I have behaved to protect myself make more sense. Placing the memories where they belong in the past removes their power to haunt my present.

May

I have no reason to fear visibility; I am delighted with who I am.

As children many of us felt invisible because we were not accepted as ourselves, or because we chose to become as invisible as possible to protect ourselves against further abuse and humiliation. It may have been safer to keep the lowest profile we could. In fact, this tactic might even have saved us, but at what great cost? For without being visible to others, it was nearly impossible to see and feel that we had substance in our own eyes.

Today I put mirrors in nearly every room and encourage myself to look at me regularly. I do not need to fear being visible to myself or others. In fact I desire to be seen and heard and fully present in every situation. When someone focuses a camera on me, I do not cringe or disappear. Nor do I need to create a "face." I simply remain whole and real and connected inside myself. My days of needing to hide away are over.

Today I honor the need to love and nurture myself.

This does not always come easy. But even if I feel guilty when I love and nurture myself, I know now that I am worthy of care and respect, and that I can be the first person to give those things to myself. The incest experience left me feeling cast out, unworthy, used for someone else's needs. Today I can guard against repeating this experience by involving myself with people who treat me respectfully. And when I treat myself respectfully, others are taught by my example.

I nurture myself by making decisions about important life changes and directions, and also by paying attention to simple details. Sometimes I tell myself in the morning, "Try to do three nice things for yourself today." I pick flowers to bring inside my house or buy them to bring home. I complete a task I have been procrastinating about such as cleaning up a room or making a phone call to a friend. These simple daily choices can change me from a person who feels unworthy and full of self-pity to someone who is grateful to have noticed her needs and taken care of herself that day.

I allow myself to be saddened by endings of pleasant journeys and leave-takings.

In my childhood when I went away to a camp or for a visit with relatives and found myself in a safe space, I was able to relax a little but then began to fill with dread as the time to leave approached. Reencountering the old tension after having let go of it seemed so painful it was almost enough to make me wish I had not given myself the relief. For I sensed I still had to go back and face further devastation in my incestuous family.

Today at the end of a journey when I encounter some of these old feelings, I need only let them pass through me and recognize they belong to the past. In my present life I have choices I make daily to create the environment I want to live in. I can relax on a vacation. I can return home and carry my more relaxed state with me. I do not deny my sadness at the end of a journey. It is a part of the whole experience.

I learn to trust the feeling and tone of my memories, even when they are so vague they could easily be dismissed.

Incest memories often begin like shadows on a distant horizon. They can be provoked by being sexual or by feeling used. They can nudge through from an image in a dream. I have a choice to cast out to their vague outlines and try to reel them in like a fish on a line. Even if I choose to do so, they may still elude me. I may reel in an empty line but still know there is something out there. The memory will come again when I am ready.

Even if a memory does not come into focus, I can believe in the integrity of my feelings. An eerie feeling or memory related to a particular area of my body being stimulated tells me something invasive happened there. If I cannot remember who violated me, that does not discredit the feeling; I have absolutely no reason to construct a painful reality that disrupts my ease. I will share my memory fragments with others and let them believe me until I can believe myself.

I will not stop at talking the talk of self-care but will demonstrate I mean it with my actions.

It is so much easier to talk self-care than to practice it. Of course three balanced meals a day would feel nourishing. So would working just the right amount, then taking time to relax and play. So would sleeping plenty. So would a daily spiritual practice and regular exercise. But most of us do not have the agility of a juggler. And even if we did, life constantly throws us the odd ball.

I have the willingness to take good care of myself, yet I am learning how to meet the challenges of doing it. Life always presents a glut of possibilities. Even if I establish a firm schedule for trying to live a balanced life, true self-care will require my checking in to see if this is meeting my needs today. Without flexibility and spontaneity, I am likely only to bind myself in. Even a balanced plan followed without consideration for the moment can become deadly. I choose to care for myself in a way that is enlivening. I can tune in and know what will make it so from day to day and moment to moment.

I allow myself to be vulnerable and note that in my life today this does not mean I am allowing myself to be victimized.

All of us need to be open to our vulnerability. It teaches us our limits as humans. If I plunge headlong in one direction without regard to my other needs, I will only end up hurting myself or creating a crisis. If I respect my vulnerability, I may get the input I need to slow down or take better care of myself.

Because the incest I suffered was so deeply wounding to my sense of self-esteem, I needed to split off from my vulnerability. I tried to toughen myself against feelings that told me how hurt I was. I put up an invulnerable wall to try to communicate to my perpetrator to stay away from me. This was necessary for my survival, though it may not have stopped the incest. And my vulnerability still came out, but in unconscious ways such as illness or being accident-prone.

Even though I know these walls no longer serve me, it may be extremely uncomfortable for me to dismantle them. I envision the balance and openness that vulnerability will bring me. I begin little by little to open a window to it. When I am ready, I share it with others who treat me respectfully. I note that my heart feels good when I do this and rather than being injured, I am healed.

*I give myself time for meditation; it centers me
and restores my relationship to my being.*

My response to the abuse I received was to
busy myself frenetically to stay away from the
feelings I couldn't bear to feel. This took me far
from my center, away from a healthy relationship
with my self. I became a doer, dependent on the
achievement of tasks and goals to validate my existence. I often overdid this without regard for
the needs of my body or my spirit.

Meditation is one of the practices of my healing. Whether through reading, while jogging, or
doing some other self-focused exercise—in for-
mal sitting meditation or in time spent on my
knees praying—I do it in the way of my choosing. I become quiet and focus on the simple fact
of my existence. I am aware of my breathing as a
life force. I am aware of my being as a precious
presence. I listen for the guidance of my higher
power. I allow myself to be.

I will receive the love of my friends and allow
this to secure me instead of exerting control.

In my childhood I tried to substitute control for the love that was missing. It seemed the only way to draw a sealed barrier around me that I could fill up. But it was always an illusion. I was never filled up this way. I might have achieved a feeling of some order and safety, but I was not without longing.

As I grow stronger and make more contact with my inner child, I can address her specific needs. I can recognize her control efforts and be sorry for the emptiness that came when those efforts failed to fill her, despite her heroic and unfailing work to try to get "enough." I can let her relax now and show her I am learning other ways that truly do fill me.

I value greatly the love of my friends and sister survivors, many of whom are traveling a parallel journey to mine. I trust their love for me and allow it to give me a feeling of security and strength.

I deserve the loyalty of others and will neither betray them nor tolerate betrayal.

Repeated betrayals have happened in my life. I was conditioned for betrayal by being abused as a child. Then, even though I was powerless, I may have confusingly felt as if I were responsible or "bad" in some way that caused me to be betrayed.

The truth is that an important person who had power over me betrayed me. I needed to believe that person loved me. This breach of trust led to my confusing belief that love is always accompanied by betrayal.

Today I know I deserve loyalty. I will be loyal to myself by exerting judgment and questioning others when I feel they might be betraying me.

I mourn the neglect I encountered from my parents so that I am free to lovingly support my children and other people.

One form of abuse is neglect. If I had parents who were there but not really there, spaced out on their own addictions, or consumed by their own needs, I did not receive nurturing attention. I was too young to understand I was being neglected, so I felt simply as if I were nonexistent, or as if I was a nuisance or unwanted. I also felt as if I could get away with things since so much went without notice.

In my own parenting I wish to give loving attention to my children. I need to consciously create structures for them that show I notice their behaviors and that contain consequences to teach them to be accountable. I acknowledge the feelings of abandonment that came from being neglected when I deserved to have good parenting. I mourn for my inner child so that she will find solace and I will see clearly how not to perpetuate this into another generation. I seek to find a balance rather than reacting in the opposite extreme and becoming smothering.

*I will use my stamina as an asset, but not let it
keep me going endlessly round and round in an
abusive situation.*

I learned stamina as a response to the hopelessness I felt about my childhood situation.
When I was knocked down, emotionally or physically, I got back up and began going forward.
Then I was knocked down again and the cycle
continued. I became very durable, capable of going on despite great odds.

As I heal I realize that my stamina is an asset I
can put to good use in the stick-to-itiveness required to wade through my past. On the other
hand, I must guard against being overly tolerant
of abusive situations. I often repeat the same behavior many times before realizing it is not allowing a successful result. Meanwhile, I am being
hurt by repeated disappointment and rejection. I
can be sensitive to these injuries before amassing
large numbers of them and can use this sensitivity to alter my sights or directions.

Today I reap what I sow by being present in the moment; I touch the earth and it grounds me.

The earth is my unconditionally loving mother. I need to touch her and let myself feel my connection to her. When I was abused as a child, I went outside as often as possible, sensing she would hold me, ground me, and save me from my despair with her beauty and structure.

If she was a principal source then in getting me through, she is a principal source now in healing me and teaching me to be joyful. I hoe and rake and sift her through my hands, and remember how delighted I was as a child to play in the dirt. I plant seeds without rushing on to the next moment or imagining the vegetables that will grow from them. I cover them up. I tamp the soil. I am one with the great mother. I let myself *be*.

I will take comfort in the decision I made to turn myself over to the care of the force I understand as God.

It is never easy for an incest survivor to let go of her or his will. It seemed my only hope of feeling some control. By holding strongly to my will, I could delude myself with the notion that I could steer myself to safety and comfort. But while this kept me busy, it never brought me peace of mind, security, or a sense of well-being. It always seemed as if I needed to accomplish one more thing to feel satisfied, find one more missing ingredient to add to the soup to make it perfect.

When I made a decision to turn my will and my life over to the Goddess of my understanding, I felt as if I was literally on a cliff edge. I had to pray to let go, to surrender. I had to distinguish surrender from submission. But once I did so, I felt immediate relief. The burden of being in charge lifted; I felt lightened. I began to reexperience the ease with which I find guidance when I am willing to open myself to surrender and acceptance.

*I will stand up for myself and not allow others
to exploit me as was done in my early years.*

I am nobody's doormat. When others trans-
gress my boundaries, I will stand up and fight for
myself. It is not okay that I was forced to submit
to exploitive treatment as a child. That does not
make me tainted and deserving of further ill
treatment as fitting to my lot in life.

Today I have resources with which to fight
back. I can refuse to agree with someone for the
sake of peacemaking if the peace is going to be at
my expense. I can acquire legal counsel or other
types of expert advice to determine my rights in a
given situation. I can talk to people who understand my history of victimization and allow them
to help me distinguish my feelings about the past
from what is taking place at the moment. I do not
need to fog out. Quite the contrary! By staying
aware, a threatening situation can turn into a
marker of my progress, and show me how much
I have learned a new, affirming attitude.

*My character defects call on me to dive down
into them and then rise to work with them.*

We who have been abused may feel tainted
and defective, as if parts of ourselves have been
cut out or were always missing. We are often
plagued by the feeling that our defectiveness
might have somehow brought on the incest. We
may be driven toward perfectionism as a way of
trying to keep closed the door to our defects.

In my recovery it is important to distinguish
the lie about my inherent defectiveness from my
ability now to identify my real character defects. I
need to allow myself to become part of the human race and to recognize that life doesn't draw
me toward perfection but completion, which requires interaction with my defects.

Only when I recognize a defect and realize
how it is making my life unmanageable do I work
on it so I can let it go. Then I begin to see how it
has served me and why I am reluctant to part
with it. My anger may be such a defect. Or my
silence. My work and recognition fill me out with
roundness on the journey toward completion.

Privacy is my privilege and I am my own gate-keeper. I can determine how much I need.

I am fully entitled to choose what I want to disclose and what I want to keep to myself in any relationship. I do not need to feel guilty for choosing to share or not to share according to my intuition and desire. But since my privacy was repeatedly invaded in my incestuous childhood, I did not grow up with a clear sense of how to make choices about privacy.

I need to practice making choices that respect my right to privacy so that I do not repeat what I learned in my family. This may mean closing a door, ending a conversation before the other party is ready to, or saying when I need more emotional space and then taking it. Requesting time away from my partner is also a legitimate thing to do. I do not need to fear it will be interpreted as a failure of my ability to love.

In my family of origin, love was confused with having no boundaries or allowing them to be frequently invaded. I need not relive that belief today. I am free to change my attitude and outlook, and seek the help of others in recovery who can help me see my way.

I meditate on the splendor of my womb. It softens and feels like a bloom.

Long ago the heart of my womb closed off to protect against invasion. Clang went the prison door. I locked others out, but it was not possible to do that without also locking myself in.

Even now I assume certain body postures that keep my womb in a dark prison cell. I clamp my legs together. I hold muscle tension in my pelvis and lower body. I block myself from experiencing sexual feelings except when being directly stimulated.

In my healing I meditate on my womb. I remind myself it belongs only to me. It is a well from which my spiritual, creative, and sexual energy springs. It is a well of abundance, always ready to bloom. One day at a time I let myself experience it as a treasure.

*I am worthy of recovery; I am worthy of joy
without fear of disaster.*

I derived feelings of worthlessness from being
abused. My world became shrouded with cur-
tains of doom. When something that promised
joy or success came my way, I looked eagerly toward it, perhaps I even began to open to its possibilities, but often the other shoe dropped and I
was squelched. I then developed an internal
monitor that warned me away from moving toward anything that might be good because I
could be punished for it in the end.

In recovery I see that long after the abuse is
over, I still live under the iron rule of this monitor, living a joyless existence to satisfy it. I see
that hanging on to the belief that I am unworthy
leads me to create situations that tend to confirm
it. No matter how many of these situations I have
created in the past, they do not prove me unworthy. They prove me to be injured, still applying
bandages to old wounds.

I build my self-esteem slowly by developing a
loving relationship with myself. I affirm my worthiness and open myself to joyful feelings.

I let self-love be the medicine that heals me.

I was born in a state of love and knew this feeling of worth and harmony in my heart before I could even walk and talk. I lost it soon after, however, when someone else projected their disgust onto me. My struggle in recovery is to re-open to that flow of pure and simple love for myself.

I celebrate each of the steps of my growth as I take them. When I have a burst of self-love, it might feel uncomfortable to let it in. It might be easier to turn to someone else and attribute my good feeling to them. But I need to validate that this feeling is within me and that I deserve to contain it rather than give it away. It is lovely to be able to share love with others, but I need to be mindful against seeking someone to project my love onto, and instead realize it as a measure of my wealth.

When I feel displaced, I will locate myself from my center.

As a child I was displaced. My room was invaded. My body was invaded. I was treated as a nonentity. I was not given a basic respect that would have reinforced my sense of well-being.

Now when I am overwhelmed by someone's aggressive energy, or when my space is invaded physically or verbally, I easily lapse into feeling powerless, unable to recognize and assert my rights. I must be prepared to call up at these times the knowledge that I am fully capable of protecting myself. It is okay for me to walk away from situations in which I feel abused. I will put aside worries about the outcome of my action and stick to first things first—protecting myself against further injury.

I no longer need to be displaced or displace myself to accommodate someone else's feelings or problems. When I feel like I must, I will stop, attend to myself by prayer and meditation, and reach out to others who can remind me of how to center myself.

*In my meditation or prayer, I seek the guidance
to follow the path that satisfies my purpose.*

Incest distorted my sense of having a purpose,
for in the way I was abused, the sanctity of my
being was violated. Some small voice in me cried
out, "This is wrong!" Yet because there was no
reinforcement for this voice, it was overwhelmed
by the message, "You are here to be used by
others."

As I heal I learn to correct this distortion and
find support for the view that I am here to fulfill
a distinct purpose. Listening to others share how
they have come to believe in a power greater than
themselves, I learn that prayer and meditation are
ways I can receive solace and guidance as I walk
my path. There are no mistaken directions. Even
if I reach a dead end, it does not mean I took a
wrong turn, only that I followed something until
I learned what I needed, then was redirected.

It is exciting to come into myself and my purpose at any given moment—whether it be to
share my love with others, to come to my work
with 100 percent of my attention, or to reexperience painful memories of my childhood so that I
may no longer be corralled by them.

*I seek the qualities of resilience and fluidity, and
water is the element that teaches me to flow.*

. As a child growing up in an abusive environment, I became alert to any sign of danger. I
learned to keep my antennae up at all times.
While this may have helped me feel somewhat
protected, it blocked me from flowing with my
feelings of the moment. It blocked me from playfulness. It blocked me from sadness.

Today I seek the pleasure of being truly with
myself in each moment. This means letting go the
walls of rigidity, of attachment to those old notions of safety and security.

I watch the river flowing. I realize the cells of
my own body are 80 percent water. Nothing
needs to be as fixed and rigid as I tried to make it.
I can have pools in which to linger and examine
things closely, but I need not stop the flow. The
river goes on and on until she opens into the sea.
My spirit also is at one with the larger universe. If
I relax I become a floater rather than a sinker,
held up by the flow of water around me.

I will allow myself the freedom to be playful every day.

Play expresses the lighter side of me. It is sometimes difficult for me to be playful for just this reason. In my childhood I was exposed to others' dark sides. My home was not a safe place to gather myself and let my defenses down. On the contrary, it was an oppressive place; becoming light in it felt dangerous because it might make me vulnerable to abuse.

As an adult I am now free to build a safe home for myself, both an inner home and an outer home. I recognize that life contains both lightness and darkness, and I need not wait in a constant state of readiness for tragedy to strike. Playfulness is a state of mind I can cultivate by allowing myself daily laughter and taking pleasure in small things. I will let go of tension and allow my inner child to enjoy my life as it is now. I will reserve time for play. I will be mindful to bring a playful attitude into many moments throughout the day.

Though there is great turmoil and conflict, even war going on in the world, I remain faithful to my belief that peace is possible, both within and without.

Even in the midst of the turmoil of my childhood I found moments of peace in which I was treated to a restful harmony. I found these moments in nature, in play, and sometimes, though rarely, in the company of a trustworthy adult such as a teacher, a neighbor, the mother of a friend. But because the atmosphere of turmoil by far predominated over the sense of peace or well-being, I became habitually aware of doom and dissension. I must repeatedly let go of this in order to develop a belief system that lets me focus on peace.

I learn again and again that peace is mine to choose. This does not mean I can remain in a constantly peaceful state. I encounter turmoil when I am confused, when I am challenged by others, or when I am in a flashback to an earlier painful time. But as long as I am honest, I can allow myself peace even at these times by accepting myself exactly as I am rather than taking on more armor. Especially during times of war and international discord, my belief in peace is the truth that can help me keep my balance.

I deserve all the support I need to move from being a victim to being a survivor and beyond that to being a victor.

Because I was abandoned or abused by authority figures in my childhood, it is hard for me to trust now that I can ask for help and receive it. I felt the safest way to survive was to go it alone. But I realize now my higher power often works through other people and I do not need to spend my life as a loner. I was harmed by some people, but now others are there to help me if and when I seek them out.

I may function best initially with a group of other recovering incest survivors. Or I may require more individual attention than I can get from a group. I may need to find a therapist with whom I can work. I respect my intuitive feelings as I explore these needs, allowing myself to shop around until I feel safe with someone. I take my time to slowly build trust in the person, recognizing I am particularly tender when it comes to authority figures. I allow myself to be and feel supported in my struggle and am grateful for the relief of not having to do it alone.

I am inspired by the bravery in my sister survivors' stories.

Sometimes we hear a particularly hard story—a young woman of twenty who ran away from home at fifteen to escape brutal rapes by her father. Out of her desire to protect her younger sister, she went the whole route of pressing charges, taking her father to court, and seeing him convicted. We wonder where she got the courage. We see she is a wounded human being, like us, and yet she marched through these events with a steely strength while we might be having trouble getting our head out from under the covers in the morning. And now she still must begin to pick up the emotional pieces.

I am inspired by the brave actions each of us take, large and small, on a daily basis. I see how often even our survival seems like a miracle. As we choose to thrive and not only survive, I see how important it is to have the powerful examples of others to show us how they have done it. I see my sister survivors as shining stars who often light my way.

I choose to be awake, aware, and think things through as my way of taking care of myself.

In the past many of my responses were based on unconscious impulses. If I was sexually attracted to someone, it seemed as if I should act on it. I never realized it might simply be a reflection of vitality within me. I did not pay enough attention to the availability of the other person. I plunged ahead with blinders on, and if there were consequences to my impulsivity, I felt surprised, as if I were being rudely awakened.

In the abuse I suffered, I was treated as if I did not matter. My feelings and my needs were disregarded. I had no way of reconciling myself with the offense except to bend with it by internalizing the perpetrator's disregard for me. So I softened this with vagueness, by fogging out, which left me acting on my unconscious impulses.

The only way back to myself is to become conscious. The pain of this route comes from reexperiencing and mourning past loss and abandonment. The joy of this route is that my life is mine for the taking.

I grant myself contentment, relaxation, and do not listen to the voice that tells me it is dangerous to let down my guard.

Contentment does not come as a large sea on which one floats buoyantly for days or weeks at a time. Rather it comes in passing moments where the heart's turbulence is calmed.

In my childhood I so needed to defend myself that I was hardly aware of any calm. I tried to create a calm inner place for myself through fantasy or with alcohol or other drugs. I maintained a continuous state of rage as an outer crust against allowing my inner self from being invaded or demolished.

Healing comes now when I allow myself to feel moments of contentment. I bring myself to the present and look around me at the safety I've created. I realize the ghosts of my past are still often with me, yet I am able to step away from them and open my heart fully to myself and others.

*When I give full recognition and expression to
my feelings and hear someone else out as well,
a sense of resolution and well-being enters.*

So often when others cross our boundaries or
we cross theirs, we do not even understand that
we've done so. Rather than explore our part in a
conflict, we may drag out all our defenses to protect ourselves from feeling accused, or to prove
we are right, or to cling to an image of perfection.
What started as an attempt to clarify something
can easily end up as an argument in which we
discount the feelings of another and have ours
discounted.

When I realize I had no modeling in my childhood for conflict resolution, I sometimes feel
very incompetent. I've only begun to learn true
listening in my recovery, so I feel like a two- or
three- or six-year-old. In a way I *am* those ages,
and this is good reason to look for progress not
perfection.

When I let go of notions of right and wrong
and speak only to express, not to prove anything,
then I will hear the messages of the heart's
wounds, whether it is my heart or my partner's or
friend's. When the heart has been made vulnerable and expressed itself, we begin healing and
can move to a comfortable feeling of resolution.

I recognize when an abusive situation arises and turn away from it as rapidly as possible.

I cannot expect to live in a world free of abusive situations. But as I recover, my awareness of when I am in one increases—whether I am being hurtful to myself or someone is being abusive to me. I can choose to turn away from the abuse rather than stay and reinforce old feelings of guilt and shame. I can recognize that I may be powerless over the situation and others involved in it, yet I have the power to say no to being hurt by it. I have the power to walk away with or without explanation. I have the confidence to believe what my gut feelings are telling me. I do not have to be swayed by competing voices.

Sometimes I turn away from an abusive situation only to find that I am picking away at myself internally, as if I must still be punished, as if at the bottom of it I must have been wrong or I would not have been abused. If I allow this to continue, I am only hurting and weakening myself. I need to stop doubting and turn my fears over to my higher power. It is time to let the child in me heal, to let her know that she can trust me. She can only safely trust me if I diligently reject abuse.

I structure my life to practice the attitudes that reflect my current values.

My values have changed a lot in recovery. In my abusive home I had to center myself on survival. Thus I valued things like keeping the peace at any cost, not bringing attention to myself so that I wouldn't be abused, and hiding out in the spaces where I could give myself a breather by, for instance, staying in bed late with the covers over my head.

I have carried these attitudes into my adulthood and continued more sophisticated practices of the same survival methods. But my survival needs no longer have to be my focus. I can look to practices that improve the quality of my life. Because I value serenity, I practice ways of making things right with myself and letting go of the things I cannot change. Because I value connection with others, I seek to be known by coming out of isolation and sharing myself.

Lifelong habits take time and vigilance to change. Success comes more readily when I take up these new practices only for this day I am entering. Each day well lived reinforces my values and adds up to a new way of being.

June

As soon as I admit my wrongs and make amends, I am free to pass from them.

I may think I am incapable of harming others. Because I was wronged as a child, I may be so much in need of recognition for the harm done to me that it is difficult for me to see how I have harmed others. If I recognize the harm done to me for my inner child, then I will be free to look more spontaneously at how my behaviors have affected others.

Today when I harm myself or others, when I fail to practice self-restraint and lash out with feelings such as anger or jealousy and wind up with an emotional hangover, I can choose to let this go sooner rather than later. I need to make amends for harm done and see my mistakes clearly and honestly. I envision the things I need to change and how I can best do that. Then I am free to move on.

It helps no one for me to remain mired in the past. It helps me greatly to use my energy to live the way I want to today.

Taking inventory of myself can help me look more deeply inside to see who I am.

An inventory can help me learn about myself. It is up to me to choose the best way to do an inventory. I might record my history autobiographically, or I might choose to list the things I know about myself—both my weak spots and my strengths. I may discover that many of my character defects were also my tools for survival in my childhood.

I am free now to choose the aspects of myself I want to change, and I can begin to work toward seeing them more clearly. If in my inventory I record the incidents of sexual abuse and victimization that have happened in my life, it will help me to believe more firmly that the incest really happened. Then I will be able to apply my energy toward my healing and expend less on keeping track of what happened. My life will no longer repeat like a stuck record but begin to flow.

Today I release old idealized versions of the past in exchange for a sturdy stance on firm ground.

One way I survived my childhood was to create an idealized version of it. I was assisted in this by at least one of my parents' depiction of our family life to the outside world—the cover-up reality.

Long out of my family home I may still recreate versions of this idealized family among my friends and lovers. This may have an insidious effect on my sense of being grounded and able to act from a sturdy stance. For if my reality is not based on truth, it will always be vulnerable to tumbling down like Humpty Dumpty.

It feels frightening to stick to being real. I have often given myself the illusion of joy by nostalgically looking back on the idealized picture. But one day at a time I give myself a chance to stand on firmer soil. I do not avoid the fears that come with change. I allow others to be real. I allow myself to be exactly how I am.

I accept relationships as sources of learning and connection and give thanks for how much they offer to teach me.

Often through a relationship I come to see myself more clearly. Living alone, I may believe I have just about got serenity down. I am sailing along. It appears I have few bothersome character defects. I develop a relationship, move in with another person, and suddenly I am a leaky boat. Everywhere I turn, my character defects plague me. They seem to jump out tauntingly and cause lots of trouble while letting me know it is no time to get rid of them. For they are my old survival tactics and in relationships my survival buttons are pushed. In my heart I have not yet truly come to believe that two people can coexist without one taking over the other.

This old message from the incest experience still holds center stage. A relationship may illuminate for me the fact that I have not yet unfettered myself from this belief. With acceptance of where I am, I can do the work of letting go. I can share the feelings that are binding me and move to enlist the aid of my higher power who will help me become released from this distorted idea and guide me in another way.

*I allow my awareness to be healing, freeing my
actions and feelings from judgment.*

The constantly rerunning old voice that says to
me, "You are not good enough. You failed again.
You are stupid, naive. You went the wrong way.
How could you have been so shortsighted?"
might need to keep talking, but I do not have to
allow it to provoke a reaction from me. I can be
aware that it is running without stopping to engage it, without using it as confirmation that
there is something inherently wrong with me. If I
simply observe it as something passing through,
it loses its power to turn me against myself.

I seek to be aware of myself in each moment.
To breathe deeply from the belly and notice all
my attachments without becoming defined by
them. To be aware and release my feelings and
actions from judgment, I learn who I am and notice my place and right size in the universe.

I turn my attention to God or my higher self
and make a decision to believe such a force can
take care of me.

I have a choice: I can suffer through trying to figure out everything alone or I can make a decision to relate to a power greater than myself.

As an incest survivor, choosing to turn to such a power may be difficult for me to do. It goes against the grain of my efforts to stop feeling out of control by seizing control. And here I am being asked to do the opposite. I must realize that my higher power is not an authority figure like the person who abused me. My higher power is a positive and compassionate force I can call upon with positivity.

To make my higher power more concrete, I can think of this force as a power expressed in my incest survivor's group, in a higher self, in God or a Goddess, or in a bird that comes to my window. It is up to me to search out images of this force that comfort me and lead me to feel trusting of it. When I allow myself this trust, I am immediately consoled. I see myself somewhere in the stream of this lifetime and all else gains perspective.

*I will celebrate myself in times of success,
achievement, and on special days that honor
my being, such as my birthday.*

Celebration is attention paid to myself. Because of my incest experience, becoming visible enough to celebrate seems risky and causes feelings of danger and vulnerability. In the past I learned to "disappear" as a defense against these feelings. Disappearance took different forms, such as being spacy, feeling as if I were behind a gray curtain, or literally hiding from a situation that might leave me alone with my abuser.

As I grow in recovery, I see that celebrating myself is an important part of giving myself self-esteem—to accumulating my achievements and commemorating them. They can only begin to fill me if I allow myself to take credit for them. Thus, I will take the risk each time there is something large or small to be celebrated and ritually acknowledge myself. It may be the act of standing up for myself or my college graduation or my birthday. I allow myself to celebrate and notice that it feels good, even if I am also frightened by the visibility it gives me.

I appreciate the freedom of calmness and cease seeking crisis as a way of experiencing liveliness.

We may have learned in our families that the only time it was okay to express feelings was during a crisis. We may have felt so deadened by the ways we had to detach from ourselves during the sexual abuse that the only times we felt alive were during times of crisis. We may have felt strong then, competent and passionate.

In my recovery I recognize how little time I have spent in calmness, how much in turbulence. If I am such a stranger to calmness, it may feel uncomfortable to me. It may feel dangerous because not enough is happening and feelings can overtake me. Yet I will learn to trust that it is okay to have these feelings and let them pass through. This gives a richness to my life that never came in turbulence.

Today I will depose from power the self-sabotaging voices in my head.

Today I will not drag along behind me the wagonload of burdens I acquired as a child. I see they are only encumbrances. If voices in my head argue that I am not allowed to cut loose this wagon, I will recognize this as those voices' last-ditch effort to hold me in check, to hold me away from becoming my fullest self. I will recognize that I was given a time and place on this planet by my higher power, and I have all the equipment I need to learn to give and receive love if I connect with the force I understand as God. I do not need to be perfect, only human. Perfectionism can be a form of self-sabotage, for how can I ever be satisfied if my expectations demand that I be beyond human?

Often just as things are going well, I have needed to pull a plug somehow to relieve anxiety, for I had the underlying fear that soon something would go wrong. Creating a crisis was one way of feeling as if I had some control. I can give up this behavior now; it does not serve me well in my adult life. I learn instead to sit quietly when I am troubled and trust time to shed light on my problems.

I define myself from an inner core of self-respect and knowledge and am not swayed by each and every rejection.

No one goes through life without encountering rejection. I move toward a person who doesn't respond with equal enthusiasm, I apply for a job and am not chosen, I submit my art work and it is not accepted. Are these rejections about me? Or are they simply indications of a mismatch between myself and the other?

Because in my abusive family I did not have respect and support for the development of how to accurately judge myself, I am particularly prone to interpreting rejections as negative judgments, as if they must surely be reflections of my worth. They are not.

When shopping I select something that looks good on the hanger. If I try it on, I often discover it is not right for me at all. I then simply return it to the clothing rack and think no more about it. There is nothing wrong with the piece of clothing. It simply didn't match my needs. Can I apply this attitude to other areas of my life and give myself the freedom to reject what does not fit me? As I learn to take this freedom, I will also be able to accept rejection with greater ease.

*Even when my self seems to fall into fragments
as I shatter the myth of my family, I know that
my spirit is whole and was never truly broken.*

I may never fully understand how I preserved
the intactness of my true self while it appeared I
was deadened or at least reduced to the smallness
of the head of a pin. As I recover I am continually
surprised at the tenacity of my spirit.

When I begin to examine the perilous foundation of my family and sift through the memories
of what actually happened versus the idealized
version that was presented to the world, I may
feel as if I am falling apart and becoming part of
the debris. As I pull loose bricks out of the faulty
foundation, many beliefs will tumble down at
once. I fear that I will never come together again.

But a waterfall can be my model. I watch the
water race over the edge of the rocks and break
apart midair, exploding from its old form, landing at the bottom in a mass of turbulence. I notice that a few feet beyond the landing, the water
again finds its fluid form and flows quietly on
down the river, as I will.

Beating or berating a child is sadistic; I discipline my children with respect.

There is a long history of belief in the notion that a child's will should be broken. This has been professed and practiced by many religious leaders and is often justified with biblical references. Both physical and sexual abuse have been practiced in the name of the child's purported need to be disciplined. The child who resists submission is believed to require even greater punishment. Children have been repeatedly and sadistically beaten and humiliated, even killed by people using this justification to force them to obedience. This theory has encouraged some adults to act out their uncontained urge to have power, thus perpetuating the cycle of abuse rather than forcing the adults to examine their own pain.

I recognize there is no justification for using violence or humiliation to discipline my children. My job as a parent is not to break anyone's will. It is to show respect for the needs of my children at the same time I set clear limits for them.

I will pace myself according to my needs and honor the timing that intuitively exists within me.

One way to be my own person is to honor the pace representative of my nature. Each of us needs a certain amount of quiet, reflective time. Each of us moves at a different speed. If I let others override my timing, I will become harried and out of harmony. This may arouse memories of the incest, in which I was not considered but dominated.

When relating to others, it is often necessary to accommodate the pace of more than one person. This will not hurt me or mean I am being dominated as long as I put forth my needs and desires and agree to the solution set forth. If I say yes when I really mean no, I will feel revictimized. When I feel this way, I need to recognize that this is of my own doing, identify it as a mistake that can lead me to resentment, and let it go. I will resolve to do no further damage to myself and let the experience improve my awareness for the next time. As I practice checking in with myself, I will know when I am fully able to give a true yes or no.

*Giving time and effort by volunteering to help
my support group reinforces my recovery and
offers lessons in practicing commitment.*

One aspect of my recovery as an incest survivor is to learn to take charge and make sure the resources I need for support exist. This might mean taking a turn at chairing a meeting, or even being prepared to start a new group. In the early stages of recovery, it was hard enough simply to speak out, acknowledge, and share about my incest. Each time I did so, I encountered the boomerang effect of my perpetrators' voices telling me I shouldn't have. Nonetheless I found it empowering and continued in spite of the voices.

When I am ready to do service, I discover that it can validate my commitment to recovery. It is a gesture to show the opposing voices that no matter how loudly they speak, I will not negotiate with them. I realize how much I've learned about my recovery path by sharing it with others. Generosity benefits me in ways I cannot predict. Hoarding contracts me and blocks my vision of abundance.

I choose to be a member of communities that affirm me, and I do not give up my sense of individuality to participate in them.

In my abusive family, the requirements for loyalty were such that they did not accommodate or promote my individual development. The needs of the controlling member or members of the family came first and obscured everything else. Because of this I may fall prey in a community to feeling as if my job is to cooperate in meeting the needs of others more than it is to meet my own.

In recovery I work to stay free of revictimization in every situation. If I have retreated from society in order to do this, I can reenter on my own terms. We all need community and connection with like-minded others. When I desire this I will go forth to claim it. I may start first in the safest places, making community with other sister survivors who are recovering. But, as I grow stronger, I will fulfill my desire to go in different directions as well, joining groups that represent my interests.

I no longer need to keep the secrets; I lighten my burdens by sharing them.

Keeping a secret is a burden. My first secret may have been an incest incident. Damaging as this experience was, the damage spread even more widely as I learned to make secrets of my thoughts and feelings.

In my healing I have the opportunity to come out of hiding. I may feel as if I dare not attempt it—that some long-hidden aspect of myself will not be acceptable to God, other people, or to myself. This feeling comes from my pride, my perfectionism, my need for control—all traits that have given me the illusion of safety until now.

When I am ready to share my secrets, I will discover that I am fully acceptable in my humanness. That another human being can accept me as I am will leave me feeling light, as if a load has been lifted off my back. I will discover that by telling my story, I see myself more clearly and feel known.

Resentments are poisonous. I make the choice to let go of them daily.

Even if for many years I've protected myself by clustering resentments around my heart, it is not too late to realize my delusion. While these resentments are held to injure others who have injured me, it is I who suffers from their toxicity. And it is I who has the power to let them go.

I feel exceedingly frightened about giving up the only means of protection I was able to grasp as a child who suffered incest. As I recover, my heart's desire to open becomes more and more present. I find myself on a fence, wanting to step into the peaceful meadow, leaving the battlefield of my past behind, but too afraid to let go of the resentments, as if that would leave me barren and unprotected.

I ask my higher power for guidance, and trust it is in this power greater than myself that I can find the care and solace I need for healing. My wounds become more exposed as my resentments drop away. Rather than seeing that as a dangerous situation, I see that I have a better chance to touch and heal them.

When I admit my powerlessness over things not within my control, I free my energy to change those things I can change.

It has not been easy to admit that I was powerless over the abuse, for I always thought I would make myself feel better by snagging some power over it. I tried to do this by taking some responsibility for it, as if I were a guilty party. I tried to do it by seeing myself as the powerful secret keeper, protecting the perpetrator from exposure. I have gone to any lengths to avoid letting myself drop off into what I perceived as the ultimate powerlessness.

Yet when I am exhausted from my efforts to negotiate with the nonnegotiable and control the uncontrollable, I finally arrive at the crossroads of surrender. It feels frightening to reverse direction from a lifetime of dogged effort to control. But when I do, I find there is no vacuum at all but a deep well of feelings—my sadness, my rage, and my hope. I feel at one with the truth and I know a power greater than myself is with me on this journey. I have the freedom now to pursue the things that I can change.

Confusion about sexual pleasure is a natural result of having been stimulated in a molesting situation.

Our very first awareness of our body as a source of sexual pleasure may have come when we were molested. We didn't like being held down or made hostage in whatever way we were. We didn't choose to be molested. We didn't even choose to have our body respond, yet it is okay if we did like the discovery of pleasure in our body. This is our God-given gift to enjoy. It is unfortunate that we became aware of it while in a devastatingly powerless situation.

Today, at times, I still become confused when sexual feelings are present. I suddenly feel like wires are crossing, short-circuiting my brain. I feel powerless and submissive to the person who is provoking the feelings, as if I am intoxicated and must lose my good judgment. It is important for me to give myself time for the confusion to pass, as I would with any other stimulus. I do not need to cut myself off from pleasure. Neither do I need to respond until my head is clear.

I choose to let positive attitudes lighten my being today.

The incest I suffered as a child exposed me to a very dismal view of life. This and the burden of keeping the incest secret contributed to my becoming shrouded in negative attitudes. If I declared all life to be hellish, what more could disappoint me? I was in pain and since no one recognized it, I thought I would betray myself if I left it even for a moment.

Today I know that even when I am in pain I can adopt positive attitudes. I can be grateful to be able to touch my feelings. I can be grateful that I have friends with whom to share them I know that I have been wounded by my past experiences, but I am not solely those wounds. I am also the person who is healing. As I recognize the pain of the past, I am able to begin to experience life in a new way. I am able to love myself and others. I am able to know the abundance of my spirit and live my days one at a time with the knowledge that I am cared for. When I find myself lapsing into the negative, I have the choice to turn myself around and alter my experience simply by perceiving things anew, as if through a different lens.

Each disappointment is a little death. I let my-self feel each loss and also know the feeling will pass with time.

In the betrayals of my childhood abuse, I en-countered major disappointments. I was repeat-edly seduced and abandoned. I was set up to compete for attention in a way that implied it was attainable when in fact it was always just out of reach or hitched up with abuse. Given this atmo-sphere, I needed to live on a narrow track, min-imizing the possibilities for feelings to come through. I protectively took the attitude: "If I ex-pect nothing, I won't get hurt or disappointed."

As I heal and allow my life to become more spacious, I am bound to encounter disappoint-ment when things don't go my way. At first I feel devastated beyond what seems appropriate to the circumstances. It seems as if I am emerging as a spoiled brat, overly demanding. But if I stay close to my desires and acknowledge that something did not go as I wanted and that was a loss to me, the disappointment will pass through me. I will be left unscathed and with my larger world in-tact. I can remain mindful that to experience the now I need not recycle the past.

My body and spirit are part of the larger creation and my purpose on this planet is to continue in that blooming.

The birth of each of us was a pure creation. Those of us who were abused and neglected in childhood often felt misplaced, as if we were not meant to be here. Otherwise, why would we have been treated so badly? But this was a necessary delusion that helped us survive until we could see and believe differently.

As I begin to recover, I become responsible for my place on this planet and the belief in the dignity of my being. I move toward fulfilling the purpose that feels right to me. One step at a time, I empower myself to do and be all that I am meant to.

I am a full citizen of the world. I take part in constructing and creating a healthy planet. I refrain from using the abuse done to me as an excuse for acting on destructive impulses. Instead, I turn to constructive ones that focus on my healing.

I am entitled to fulfilling my sexuality.

As a survivor of sexual abuse, my responses to sexual pleasure have been contaminated. It feels like wires cross in my brain. When I first became aware that sexual abuse occurred in my childhood, I felt very defensive about sexual intimacy and had little desire to be sexual with anyone. I even wondered, "Why would anyone ever want to come close enough to touch another person? How did this sex stuff ever get started anyway? And why does it continue?" But as my recovery progressed, my desire for intimacy and sexual connection sprouted new life. It was with fear and trepidation, but I gradually became sexual again with the guidance of my incest recovery group and therapist.

Today I can enjoy a sexual relationship and claim my pleasure as my own. I can release the notion that if I allow myself enjoyment and fulfillment, I will be handing my power over to another person. Still, my feelings vary depending on how vulnerable I feel. There are times when the voices in my head try to make me feel as if someone else has entered the bedroom besides my lover. I am free to stop at any time during sex to discuss this and, in this way, expose those invaders.

I let go of my hard and fast clinging to ideas of what should happen and move into the flow of life.

We all have a natural impulse to contract around pain. Scar tissue grows from the sides of a wound inward until it meets in the middle. It covers the wound but is thin and brittle and rigid. My psychic scars have been covered over with fabric of a similar quality.

At this point in my development, rigidity has ceased to serve me well. I visualize replacing it with greater elasticity. In rigidity I try to predict the next moment, the next day, the next relationship, so that I can perceive I have some control over it. But instead of guaranteeing any certainty, I merely succeed in squeezing the life out of the now.

I am free today to choose to move into the flow of life, trusting my higher power has some design. And I am free to participate instead of taking charge.

When I am at home in my body and in the now, vitality trickles into me like an infusion of spirit.

My vitality was never really lost, though I may have felt trampled and as if I could not reach it because I was too afraid to come home to my body. I have to honor how I left my body as the survival tool it was. I may have turned to alcohol or other drugs in the belief that I could find vitality in some outwardly induced high, but this was not my true liveliness.

Today in my healing I realize vitality is within me. Sometimes when I am uncomfortable with what I have to learn, I still try to exit from my body. I burrow into the past or obsess on the future. I turn off from recognizing the feelings my body tries to communicate, such as exhaustion, hunger, anger. I set out to analyze all the complications and ramifications of a problem rather than simply tuning into my heart and listening.

When I feel flat, I will knock on my own door, asking, "Are you home in there?" If I hear no answer I will go look in a mirror and talk to myself until I become present. My spirit will rise as I realize I am home free.

*My dreams are valuable resources that enliven
and inform me.*

As abuse survivors many of us have been
plagued with nightmares. We may have trouble
sleeping or feel anxious about the approach of
night. If we have been tormented by our dreams,
it is not surprising that we might want to reject
them. But they are valuable resources. We need
them. We need to learn ways to make sense of
them so that they do not hold the power to shake
us down with fear.

I discover that writing down my dreams lets
me begin to get a handle on them. It also helps to
tell a "bad" dream to someone else. Even when I
am mystified by its meaning, as I tell the dream I
feel it losing some of its power to haunt me. After
I have written or told my dream, I can ask myself
what I associate with its symbols. I may begin to
gain insight. Even if I don't, if I save the dream
and look back on it later, I may discover that it
reveals itself quite clearly.

As I become more understanding of my
dreams, I discover that they are not all dreadful.
Many of them provide me with sustenance. Some
of them lead me to the locus of my energy.

I will feel the sadness of my loss when I need to separate from friends because of moving or because of paths otherwise diverging.

Good friends are treasures. They nurture me with enthusiasm and help me reflect on myself with their honest feedback. They become a constellation around me, a network in which I feel located and oriented. They do not define me but work positively for me as part of a support system I have built.

When I must leave friends, I feel sadness and loss. Though we may still love each other, I need to mourn the loss of their presence. I am not ready to make new friends until I open myself to this process, for we are each unique and none of my friends are replaceable. As I allow myself to grieve I feel my aloneness, my separateness from all other beings. I may be frightened to feel this because of my incest, because when trust was broken in my childhood I was thrust involuntarily into isolation.

Today I can sit still with my losses, letting the appropriate sadness reside in my heart until it is ready to pass on and open me to new friends.

*I put the strength and tenacity I developed as a
child to good use for myself.*

I developed a steely strength and durability by
sustaining myself through the threatening situations of my childhood. My tactic was to split off
my tough surviving side from my injured side
that told me I was crumbling. As I enter recovery,
I fear that if I bring out my vulnerability, I will
have no power, no tenacity. Yet I have plenty, if
only I can integrate the part that sustained me
with the vulnerability.

Our strengths might have lain in silence, or in
aggression, or in imagination. We are free now to
remove them from their old forms and see them
simply as part of our fabric.

I consciously choose to transform my strength
to be able to use it directly for my benefit. In
stressful situations, if I lapse back into old patterns that no longer serve me, I stop a moment
and focus on reintegrating myself, remembering
I do not wish to sacrifice my wholeness for
anything.

When I truly cease to believe I deserve deprivation, I begin to receive what is mine.

I felt ashamed as a child. I was too young to know not to absorb the attitudes put on me by my parents who blamed and shamed me. The consequence of living in this shame-based condition was grave deprivation, for as long as my insides told me I was undeserving, it was difficult to allow myself to knock at any door except the one that would be slammed in my face.

Today as I recover from shame, my eyes are opening to the many other doors I can choose. I look around at my relationships and realize I can let go of the ones that are empty. I know I deserve to receive love and to have my love received by others. As shame drops away, I am amazed at how many doors I can reach through and how often I am met when I do so.

*Today I know I deserve to stand up for myself
and have my needs met.*

I was taught to protect others rather than stand
up for myself. It remains difficult for me to state
my needs, purely and simply, without ambivalence. As a child my needs were not validated.
They were trivialized or disregarded. I did not
learn that it was okay for me to seek ways to meet
them. I was trained to take the crumbs, to believe
myself unworthy of first-class citizenship.

Today I have learned that I must stand up for
myself if I wish to build my self-esteem. Further-
more, I know that it feels good when I get my
needs met. I cannot rely on others to mind-read
what my needs are if I do not tell them what they
are. I am responsible for letting my needs be
known. I cannot control the outcome when I tell
others my needs, but I need to let myself be
known this way, despite the risks.

If I encounter guilt and discomfort in the after-
math of standing up for myself, I understand this
comes from voices from the past. As I move forward, sometimes these voices become even more
fierce. They fear being left behind with good reason. For without my attention, they have no life.

July

When I feel as if I am going round and round and nothing is ever going to change, I ask for the humility to know that I am just not seeing what is changing.

We each have pitfalls we repeatedly find ourselves in. They may be old defenses, unconscious escapes, or expressions of unmet parts of our inner self. For instance, we may recreate in our relationships the same abusive dynamics over and over. When we discover we have done this one more time, we may feel discouragement heaped on our heads. "Oh, no, not again."

When I feel this discouragement, it is time to mourn again for the abuses suffered as a child. I may as well understand that there is more to be learned here. I will learn nothing unless I focus on myself and realize the choices I have made. Even if my experience feels repetitive, I will see it is not. I am forever evolving. Keeping in touch with my higher power can help me have the humility I need to know my work is leading to changes, even when I cannot yet see them.

I will freely admit my errors and work to become the person I know I am capable of becoming.

Taking a close look at who I am and sharing what I see with others can help me understand myself in new and more focused ways. I used to pretend to be flawless because I feared admitting my errors would mean I had to admit fault for the incest experience. This was not so. When I stopped trying to defend my flawlessness, I began to understand which of my attitudes and behaviors made it difficult for me to feel good about myself. I had to live with this new awareness for some time before I was ready to let go of anything. It was uncomfortable to even think of letting go of those old ways because they were like a shell, my armor, and they could not easily be discarded.

In my discomfort, I often felt that there was no place to go. I thought, "It's too late to go back, yet I'm too frightened to go forward." Then I would remember that I am not alone. I would ask for the help of my higher power, remembering I am not in charge of everything. My faith would carry me past the fear, and I discovered my higher power will do for me what I cannot do for myself.

*The only true security comes from within—
from my learning to trust myself and my
perceptions.*

Because as a young child my development as a
separate person was discouraged, I had no resources with which to create inner boundaries to
define me. Instead, I became dependent on the
views and perceptions of others. I was not provided with a secure home and yet I was given the
impression that the only way to seek one was to
find someone who could create one for me.

How can I begin now to create and maintain
my separate self and learn to trust my own perceptions? First, I must get honest. If I am building myself on the one hand but lying to myself on
the other—about some addiction, memories of
my incest, or even by disputing the notion that I
am a valuable person who deserves honesty—I
will not truly establish a secure feeling.

I begin with an honest self-appraisal, treating
myself with compassion for those ways I have
needed in the past to survive. Even if it feels as if
I have little to start with, by becoming honest I
will feel safe and secure with myself and this will
be surprisingly enough.

*The person who deserves my first order of loyalty
is me.*

I was raised to give loyalty to an amorphous
mass—the family—without regard to what was
being done to me. So it is not surprising that I
have difficulty with loyalty now. I think I must
give it fiercely and unequivocally, even when the
person to whom I give it is hurting me. Or I think
if I have been loyal to someone in the past, I am
obliged to remain so forever, regardless of how
his or her attitude toward me has changed.

I was neglected in my childhood lessons about
loyalty. I was not taught to be loyal to my feelings, my intuitions, and my sense of what I
needed. Quite the contrary, I was taught to abandon my needs in the name of loyalty. Today I
have the choice to teach myself anew that my first
order of business is to consider myself.

When I act as if I deserve to be loyal to myself,
I give others the signal that I deserve to be treated
with loyalty.

The only sure way to have enough is to know that what I have is enough.

Greed has a voracious appetite, never full. Deprivation sits at the opposite pole. We who were sexually abused as children suffered deprivation when it came to love and quite possibly in other ways as well. To make up for the past, our unconscious response to deprivation may be greed. But our conscious response can be to learn how to notice when we have enough, how to let ourselves become people who can feel satisfied.

This means having the willingness to turn my negative attitude to a positive one. As I count what I have rather than what I have not, I quickly begin to know gratitude. My perspective on what can fill me broadens. For instance, if I want several books but do not have the money to buy them, I might discover that I live in a place with a fine library. When my attitude is adjusted, I realize I am missing nothing I truly need.

I recognize that life is ever-changing and allow myself to take pleasure in the vitalizing flow of its currents.

I have been too busy trying to fix life in place to take pleasure from change. My clutching for security grew out of the sexual abuse that disrupted and distorted my autonomous relationship to my body. This threw me off balance and led me to grasp at outer structures for stability, taking me away from my center and my heart.

Today when outer structures change, of course I become anxious. But I do not need to limit myself, protect myself, or have my life narrowed because of a fear of change. I can see change as vital. I do not need to change everything at once, but gradually I can change anything I want to. I can see now that struggling to hold things rigidly in place has not been a useful source of stability. I choose to center myself in my body and my spirit. I watch the current flow in a river. I watch the tide rise and fall. I, too, can flow as I seek and find my true nature.

*I am developing trust in my perceptions, needs,
and purpose.*

The environment of my abusive and dysfunc-
tional family was not one that helped me value
myself as a developing person. Rather, I was
forced to fuse with the family system of power
and subjugation, to focus on meeting others'
needs as my way of relating. My ability to develop clear perceptions and needs was stunted. I
became acutely tuned to picking up other people's needs but not my own.

In recovery I have the opportunity to place
myself in an environment that supports my developing sense of self, where others are not intol-
erant when I stick with my own perceptions,
even if this causes disagreement. Often after believing myself, I encounter a boomerang of dis-
belief in myself. When this happens I can
recognize that the old family training is trying to
make a reappearance, give it a polite nod, and get
on with the business of discovering who I am. As
I gradually become more faithful to myself, a
sense of my legitimacy and purpose grows and
fills me.

When my pain is so great I sometimes can't grasp my faith, I can let myself be carried through those days or moments by my sisters in recovery.

Faith is both a thinking and a feeling proposition. Sometimes I feel it. Other times I can't feel it but I still carry in my head the notion that it is real. I can think of no better reason for why my creator gave me intelligence than for holding knowledge in storage between the times my heart can feel it.

When we are in great pain, it becomes more difficult to be believers. This may have begun in childhood when we were first exposed to a notion of God while suffering the betrayal of a parent or other trusted person who abused us. Now that we are functioning and recovering adults, we can understand why our inner child might feel so bereft. Yet we can also comprehend that our higher power can help us through hard times.

When my own faith wavers and feels deficient, I will put myself in the company of others who can remind me that I am being guided.

I allow myself to be visible and receive recognition for my accomplishments.

In childhood, and especially in the presence of those who abused us, it was not safe to be visible. Some of us developed the sense of being invisible because we were not seen as ourselves, but as someone our abuser needed to see and use.

As I grew up and left my family, I followed a course in which I failed to recognize my accomplishments. I feared that visibility would lead to further injury. At some point I realized that this no longer serves me. It only leaves me empty and frustrated, as if all that I do goes into a bucket with a hole in the bottom of it. Nothing good accumulates.

I am worthy of praise and recognition. I allow myself to receive acknowledgment, even when it means walking through the discomfort I experience about being visible.

I am a valuable human being. To behave in a way that discounts this is to ignore truth.

In my incest experiences my basic value as a human being deserving of respect and independence was not honored. Those people in authority who were meant to teach me to value myself gave me lessons in devaluing and diminishing my worth. I intuitively sensed I deserved better, yet I internalized their view in which my self-worth was maimed.

As I heal I discover that my path is a continual search for truth. When I work through one layer of lies that has overlaid my basic nature, I come to see another layer. Once I've seen that the ways I've devalued myself have perpetuated the lie that I am unworthy, I can no longer believe this and be in unity with my higher power. It is time to see myself as entitled to a valuable and valued existence.

Shame is no longer the leading contender in my self-definition. I release its bindings and return to my innocence.

I was schooled in a shame-based family system. My family was excessively interlocked with unhealthy dependency. When I was abused, I took on the abuser's shame. I became accustomed to feeling badly about myself whenever something did not go smoothly or successfully.

If I was not loved by someone, if someone failed to notice me, if I performed publicly and the applause was not excessive, I felt ashamed. I strove to correct this with perfectionism, with inhuman expectations of rising above everyone else.

Today I can see how I reacted out of shame and release myself from these old behaviors. I give myself the gift of understanding that regardless of the responses of others, I do not need to be ashamed unless I have done something I need to make amends for. And if that is the case, I know the way to move forward from my error is by making the necessary amends. As I release my shame, I guide my inner child back to her original innocence.

I choose to stay present in my body, even for the uncomfortable feeling of exhaustion.

Those of us who learned to exit from our body as a way to escape the pain of abuse now have to learn to stay planted inside ourselves. Why not go on using this talent to go out of body when it's useful, for instance when the dentist is drilling out our cavities or when we are enduring the utter fatigue of moving from one home to another? Because we have recognized the price our escape exacted—the price of being separated from ourselves—and we have learned that we can best protect ourselves by being present and letting our feelings guide us.

When I am exhausted, I need to rest. Even if many things remain to be done, I can make a quiet space within and allow myself serenity. I do not need to be continually harried over unfinished business. I can rest and accept my discomfort until energy begins to trickle back in and my body tells me I am ready to start again.

I cannot accept feelings selectively; even despair I must acknowledge despite my fear of its darkness.

My childhood was darkened. I tried to find ways to preserve myself by looking away from the darkness. I did this through a vivid fantasy life or by creating unrealistic myths about my life and family. I did it by abusing mood-altering substances to help me exit from reality.

While these tactics may have saved me, today they block me from growing. I am learning to protect myself in a completely different way—by feeling my feelings. Anger tells me to make a little distance. Fear tells me I am threatened and must take care of myself. Joy tells me to open my heart and smile. Yet when despair comes, I am reluctant to feel it and I try to push it away. I do not trust it will pass like the other feelings; instead, I fear it will envelop me. But it only grows larger as I ignore it.

When I feel despair, I am brought face-to-face with the deep hopelessness I felt as a child. Today I have a choice and can explore this feeling, protecting my inner child as I walk through it.

Rather than being a spoiler with my envy, I turn my attention to what it shows me I want or am lacking.

I was deprived of nurturing attention as a child. I was set up to compete with siblings for what was construed to be love but in fact was the opportunity to try to fill up an empty parent. This was a no-win situation from the start, yet I mistakenly thought the failure was mine. I envied others, believing they were getting what was rightfully mine. I thought there was not enough to go around.

Today I recognize envy as an emotion that can help me see what I lack. When I become riveted to someone's successes or gains, whether they are financial rewards, good relationships, or outer approval and attention, I can look beneath my feelings to identify my desire for something similar. I want the attention I am envying or the job or the love. Once I focus on myself, I can return to a balance, bring what I do have into perspective, and begin to act to direct myself toward what I don't have but would like. My energy will be much better spent this way.

I allow the growing up of my true self to fill me.
I allow my achievements to count.

Without self-esteem, no matter how much I worked on myself or how many goals I achieved, nothing seemed to add up. I still felt empty. As soon as I accomplished something, my lacking self-esteem said, "Well, if you accomplished that, it must be nothing." Thus I was able to discount things that would have built mighty pride in someone else. While this deprived me in one way, in another way perhaps I should be grateful, for it kept me searching for the wounded part of me that needed my attention.

Now that I am giving that wounded part attention, I am beginning to fill up. I am growing to trust myself, knowing I will no longer deny my wounds. The result is that all I have done and all the strides of my growth are beginning to compute and count. There is no longer a hole in my bucket.

I will learn to respect my anger and use it appropriately.

Taught as a child that my anger was not acceptable, I learned ways to repress this natural emotion. I learned to blame others when my anger was provoked. I learned to keep it inside and abuse myself with acts of self-mutilation, such as chewing the skin on the inside of my mouth.

As I uncover incest memories, I see myself as deeply wounded. After the hurt I often feel rage. I realize my rage is old anger that had no outlet and no acknowledgment. Today, however, I can respect it. I can see that it is roused when I feel threatened, and I allow it to wake me to the need to protect myself. I can begin to express this rage to myself, a therapist, or another safe person. I can begin to discriminate between the threats of the past and the reality of today. Then I can choose to express myself appropriately to the people around me.

*I give myself time alone in which to know
myself and my higher power more deeply.*

Often other people, places, and activities are
put in my path as teachers. Still it is important for
me to spend time alone getting to know and love
myself. It is important for me to distinguish between loneliness and solitude. I am lonely when I
am set apart within myself, whether in the company of others or by myself.

In my childhood I had no way to know I was
taking up blame and shame that belonged to others who failed to own it and who exploited my
innocence by shoveling it onto me. I wound up
feeling so sure I must be a bad person that I was
afraid to look too deeply into myself, though I
yearned to be known. I busied myself to avoid it.

Today I have faced the void and found plenty
of good in me. My inner child often still takes up
the old messages and becomes afraid that to be
quiet and alone will be treachery. But I reassure
her. In solitude I honor my being and reach a
new depth of knowing myself.

I can create rituals to give attention to my passages and to clear myself of old associations and attitudes.

When significant events happen, we can choose to commemorate them in new ways. Doing so can help us reduce the influence of old patterns and associations.

During the abuse we were forced to live with the abuser's version of reality overriding ours. Our perpetrator might have used the authority of the patriarch, might have been a church-going, law-abiding, so-called upstanding pillar of the community who broke all rules only in our presence. As a result of this hypocrisy, we may feel as if we cannot trust community or the surface look of respectability.

Today I am free to create for myself a life and my own community. I can start by ritually clearing any new space I move into physically or emotionally. I give myself permission to have *my* life there, rather than living out the commands or unconscious wishes of others. I can ask others to join me as witnesses and friends, and tap the power that lies in us to create a new awareness.

*Through falling apart I am able to restructure
myself with my truth as my foundation.*

When we first admit that we were sexually
abused and open a window to the knowledge of
its effects on us, we often feel as if our world as
we have known it falls apart. We become chaotic.
We may be so disoriented that unknowingly we
cross the street on a red light instead of a green
one and nearly get run over. We may lose some
fantasy backdrop about sex and violence we long
lived with like a continuous film always playing,
rarely noted until ceased. We may become highly
emotional, crying at almost anything. We may
find ourselves seeing every touch, every gesture,
every connection between humans through the
lens of the incest we suffered.

Falling apart is frightening to anyone who un-
dergoes it. Yet I recognize its necessity and its
benefits. For I do not want to return to a place or
time in which I am shrouded with my secrets. I
learn to be patient, allowing the passage of time
to slowly offer me new perspectives. I recognize
my courage and my willingness to walk into the
wilderness, and I give myself credit for doing
whatever it takes to keep going.

I accept myself as whole today regardless of where I am in my journey.

My journey takes me down bumpy roads. Sometimes I can glimpse light a long distance away; other times I cannot see around the next corner. When I fail to accept where I am in my journey I become my own opponent and spend my time mired in resistance.

If I took on blame for abuse I received in my childhood, it is not surprising I could not accept myself. I felt like a bad person, though in my heart I did not understand how I got to be that way. The shame was free-floating. Someone else's shadow had been cast over me.

As I heal, I take on my own problems and character weaknesses and learn how to work with them. I relieve myself of the burden of false guilt, of responsibility for things that are not mine. I accept myself at each stage of my journey, whether I am feeling angry, full of grief, sad, strong, or joyful. I am capable of feeling all my feelings without them blowing me off my course.

When I feel profoundly lonely, I do my best to remember my faith in a power greater than myself. Then I am no longer inconsolable.

Sometimes I feel as if I am totally alone in this world. I realize I felt this way as a child but didn't have words for it. When I was backed into a corner by my abuser, when a molester told me all was well, that I was a good girl, I was reduced to having a small hold on reality. I tried to get far from my body. The person I needed to comfort me was often the one distorting my reality. How then could I reach out and be consoled?

Today when I am lonely it is often because I have moved away from myself. I am as apart from myself as I was back when I needed to escape the abuse. I am apart from my belief in a higher power who is guiding me in ways I am not even aware of. It can relieve my loneliness to realize I am never alone. My higher power is always with me. Sometimes my higher power works by providing another human being to speak to me or listen to me. I open myself to see and hear what I am missing.

When I have the willingness to forgive and to be forgiven, I am free to take action.

Because sexual abuse is such a grave violation, we as survivors may feel as if we will do best to stay away from forgiveness entirely. When we think of forgiveness, our mind runs first to our perpetrators. Why should we even consider forgiving them, especially if they have not made any amends to us or acknowledged their offenses?

We do not need to press ourselves about forgiveness, but we do need to be willing to feel that gentle tap our higher power sometimes gives to our shoulder. A whisper that says, "You do not have to carry this weight by holding on to hatred about everything that happened in the past."

I practice being open to forgiveness first for smaller offenses. I forgive myself for making mistakes. I forgive my friend for her or his words that hurt me. I forgive my cat for throwing up on the furniture. The longer I am open, the more clearly I will see that my liberation lies in forgiveness.

I experience awe at the delicacy and vigor of my unfolding.

Much of the awe that goes with the innocence of childhood was lost to me. Yet my child found in nature a place to continue a relationship with beauty and growth, and to witness change through the seasons. In my family's home I needed to be rigid. I felt this would give me some control over a stressful situation. But this left me only a small space in which to focus on myself and the growth and changes natural to childhood.

Today I can take as much time as I want to focus on my development. I can choose to have the relationships I desire and say no to those that I am not ready for or do not want. I can take time for rest and recovery and not feel guilty for giving myself what I need.

I can continue to be awed by nature—whether visiting the Grand Canyon or watching buds swell to open flowers in spring. I can also watch and feel the flowering inside me as I learn to enrich my soul. I can be awed at the vigor of healing.

Despite fear I speak out about injustices whenever I am able to.

Silence was my survival. It was not my choice, its source was not cowardice but the will to live. I need to remember this and respect my tenacity rather than put myself down for keeping quiet under conditions of attack. Having done that, I need to also realize that silence narrowed my world and kept me confined to a small space. I no longer choose to live in confinement. The antidote to silence is to speak out.

I speak out first by revealing the abuse I suffered to others who can be trusted. I speak out by standing up for myself when others threaten to tread on my territory. I speak out when possible to protect and defend the rights of children. Each time I speak out, I am likely to encounter fear. The child within me fears danger, even annihilation with the breaking of silence. I reassure her as I go along that I am capable of protecting her, validating her fear but showing her my adult self is present to help her be safe now.

I allow myself to compete when that mode is appropriate.

Competing can help me practice standing up for myself repeatedly. In a tennis game I need to bring myself fully to each point. If I hit a good shot, I do not need to flub the next two as an apology. As an incest survivor I am tempted to do that because when I stood up for myself in my childhood, I was knocked down again and again. Even if no one wants to knock me down now, I have an internal demon that tries to convince me that someone does.

While competition can help me to define my boundaries, I can become overly competitive and use it to avoid intimacy. Competition faces us against another person with similar skill. It draws forth all our resources and energy, but it is a singular mode with limited dimensions. I need to use it in appropriate situations, such as playing a game or when applying for a job I desire. But I need to realize there are other modes, such as asking for my needs to be met, that are more appropriate than competing, especially when it comes to an intimate relationship or a friendship.

I seek the freedom to be all of who I am and to love myself and others without reserve.

Vague and fleeting as freedom may seem to be, we all know moments when we have felt a lightening of the heart, a sense of soaring, a connection to the well of limitless joy. Our memories of these moments may be all too few and far apart, yet we do not forget them.

The freedom to explore and be, which is my birthright, has been held an arm's length away by my need to wall off and protect against invasion, which grew out of the abuse. For instance, if I fully relaxed I could be devastated if my perpetrating grandfather unexpectedly arrived on the scene. I learned to put up barriers that kept me on guard and also kept me far from a ranging freedom.

Today as I heal I come back to my original impulse to freedom. I want to own the sexual pleasure that was stolen from me. I want to be able to play freely and to fulfill all I am meant to be.

I free myself of the need to protect others and refuse guilt that does not belong to me.

Most perpetrators of abuse do not consciously carry guilt for their acts. They project it onto their victim, often a young child who does not yet have a developed understanding of responsibility. If I carried the guilt for my incest, I never learned to truly distinguish what was mine. I felt the shamefulness of another, yet I called it my own. I felt this was the way to obtain love. If my parents acted inappropriately and I protected them from seeing the inappropriateness of their actions by taking the blame for them myself, then wasn't I loveable? What I really wanted was unconditional love, but if that was not possible I would meet the required conditions.

As I recover I realize I have often taken a role in relationships to protect others rather than myself. I have thought I was promoting the peace or being a good person. I have thought I was somehow assuring that I would be taken care of. But I see now that this has guaranteed me nothing; instead I have enabled others not to confront their problems and have inflicted injury on myself. I no longer need to, nor can I afford to, take on guilt that does not belong to me.

As I acquire self-esteem from sources deep within me, I become someone who knows and communicates that she deserves loyalty.

As incest survivors, the loyalty and protection we might have expected from a parent or other important authority figure was lacking entirely or present only sporadically, then betrayed. We struggled to fit ourselves into this system in a way that would let us escape from seeing its painful reality. For instance, we may have believed that the abuse meant we were being singled out as a favorite—that we were being given an "opportunity" to fulfill the needs of someone we wanted to satisfy. It was too unbearably painful to see that we were being hurt by someone we needed to be our protector.

Painful as it is even now to recognize that I was an unprotected child who was betrayed by abuse, it is a beginning that allows me to build self-esteem and cease the cycle that perpetuates my unconscious belief that I deserve more abuse. I work to become consistently loyal to myself by regularly checking into my wants and needs and asking myself if I am taking care to meet them. I practice affirming my worthiness, my loving nature, the rightness of my being. As I develop full loyalty to myself, I am less vulnerable to the betrayal of others, for I am free to teach them how to treat me.

*When I am gentle with myself, my heart opens
and gives me direction.*

It is always a good principle to practice being
gentle with myself. I have had many years of being hard, of carrying around a punishing parent
inside me who said, "You haven't done enough
yet. . . ." "Why are you this way? . . ." "What are
you trying to get away with? . . ." "Why do you
need something now, can't you wait awhile?" It is
time to say back, "This is my life and I'll do it my
way, thank you."

Even when I promise myself that I will be gentle, this is not an easy order. For I am deeply ha-
bituated to putting myself down, to negative
thoughts and feelings. Sometimes the more
healthy I become, the more subtle and stealthy
those voices become. I can learn to recognize
their presence by my feelings of defeat and discouragement. I can also learn not to engage them
but simply to detach and let them go.

I take full responsibility for myself and expect everyone else to do the same.

In my incest experience, I was made responsible for the feelings and needs of others. This left me confused about what it meant to be responsible. I felt unworthy when it came to taking responsibility for and caring for myself. I became irresponsible as a gesture of defiance. After all, I felt my childhood was stolen from me. Because I have not yet paid enough attention to her plight in the past, the child within me sometimes refuses to grow up.

Today I recognize responsibility as the ability to respond. To be responsible in this way builds my self-esteem. It helps define who I am and reminds me to check in with how I feel. I will not have the ability to respond unless I acknowledge my feelings and take the time to be quiet and listen to my heart. Even after I have heard and acknowledged my feelings, I am not finished being responsible until I have communicated what I need to others.

My healing is contingent upon my always moving toward the light of freedom and away from victimization.

To endure abuse as a child is indeed to be victimized and traumatized. The survivor is prone to revictimization just as everyone is prone to returning to old familiar places and circumstances of their upbringing. So it does not need to be surprising or horrifying to me if I find myself in a place where I experience revictimization.

The first step is awareness. When I realize I am feeling like a victim, I can first of all intercept the impulse to dump all over myself and instead reach out a hand to my inner child and tell her once again I am sorry for her. I can then turn to righting the situation with the help of my higher power's guidance. I must do my own footwork. This may mean walking away from an abusive situation. It may mean confronting and renegotiating the terms of a relationship to allow myself to enter it with power. It may require the risk of losing others, but I only need to concentrate on staying present for me.

I take one step at a time. Whenever I falter, I reach to my sister survivors and let their strength give me the courage to go on.

August

*When I have rainy day gloomy feelings, I know
that these too will pass just as the rain does.*

An error I am prone to making that digs me
deeper into despair is assuming that feelings are
facts. When I feel as if all is lost, as if I have struggled but gotten nowhere, it is okay to feel this
through and through. But it is not okay to assume it is a fact of my reality.

As I move along in my recovery, I distinguish
one feeling from another more easily. I learn the
shades of my disappointment, the angst of my
despair, the heartbreak of my sorrow, the fire of
my anger. I learn that each of these feelings requires acceptance before I am released by it.
When I am released, I see that the facts are still
constant, yet they may seem much more manageable because I have shifted my perspective.

*I have the ability to give and receive love, and
I will open myself to feeling its flow today.*

Because I was abused by those who suppos-
edly "loved" me, I have felt confused, mistrustful,
and I even disbelieved in the existence of love
without abuse. I lived many years in a state of
self-loathing, hoping to be rescued by someone
else's love. Yet this state did not attract love, and
the very notion of being rescued was laden with
the potential of putting myself in someone else's
power and being revictimized.

When I focus on placing myself under the care
and guidance of my higher power, I begin to
leave behind this old system and receive calmer
messages about love. Even if I am young and in-
experienced at the practice of love, I realize my
innate ability to have an open heart. I have been
wounded and damaged by my incest experience,
but I was not born flawed. Today I know I am
entitled to love myself and allow others to love
me. And only when I love myself am I able to
truly love others.

I accept my worthiness, my process, and my ability to take care of myself.

Despite my painful childhood traumas, I have all I need today to care for and heal myself. One of my greatest challenges is to accept myself as I am. Since as a child I was pushed around, used, neglected, and abused rather than accepted, it will remain difficult for me to offer simple acceptance to myself. Sometimes my neediness, my distress, or my rage may make this task seem impossible.

But I begin at the beginning. Rather than trying to convert myself into an appealing person so that I can accept myself, I accept myself as someone in a condition of great distress. I offer compassion to this hurting person. I meet her need to be seen and heard. I hold her and console her and let her know she is worthy of my caring. When I have cared for her in this condition, she will be able to move on from it.

Forgiveness is a state of being I will have when
I am ready for it.

My resentment for my perpetrator may have
been the only wall I was able to erect to protect myself against becoming totally overtaken and losing
my sense of self. Resentment seen this way shows
itself serving a useful purpose, even though it
caused me to walk through life embittered.

I no longer want or need to clutch my resentments so tightly. As I unravel my memories, go
feelingly through them but keep returning myself
to the present, I realize this process can give them
a restored place and perspective without distortion. I am not dependent on my resentments. I
am free to forgive others their trespasses without
losing track of the injuries I suffered from my
abuse. I can even feel compassion toward the
abuser for the probable abuse he or she suffered
as a child.

Forgiveness cannot be used to preempt the
pain of my healing. I must wait until I am truly
ready. Then I will feel a nudge on my shoulder,
reminding me to seek the help of my higher
power to become willing to be forgiving.

Today I am building a healthy life and accumulating a history of healthy experiences.

Before I became fully conscious of the wounds caused by the sexual abuse I suffered, I accumulated lots of experience that reinforced my being a victim. I often ran on a negative track, feeling criticized and criticizing others, convinced in advance that something would go wrong. I believed I would not be able to rely on my friends, and if I had a success it would be almost immediately followed by a failure. My history seemed to confirm this reality.

Today I see what fed that redundancy. I begin with new input. I begin to count on the positive and notice how often things come out well for me. As I work to create the life I want to lead, I become conscious that I am developing a new history of accomplishment, of reaching out and finding my friends available, of opening to the guidance of my higher power, of separating love from abuse. I till the soil for a garden of self-love. I am in a continual process of planting. And some of the things I planted a year or more ago grow stronger and stronger.

*I am empowered by self-knowledge, by owner-
ship of my experiences, and by all aspects of
myself.*

Because the abuse I received was so injurious,
to survive I needed to deny it or minimize its
consequences until now. While this denial
helped me get through it, it required much of my
energy to hold it in place. It gave me a faulty
foundation to stand on. No wonder then, I felt
robbed of my power.

As I heal I uncover my true self and the events
of my history. I find a system to support me so
that I can penetrate my denial and come to know
myself. My memories are painful and bring up
uncomfortable feelings such as rage and deep
sadness. Yet as I walk through these feelings and
find safe places to express them, I am comforted.
For I am owning all I have been through, all that
has formed me. This journey is my movement toward wholeness. I am empowered by taking it,
and in it I find love for myself.

I let go of the outcome of any given situation and allow myself to be with whatever today brings.

I cannot control many things in life. It is a relief to know this, although it often feels as if I do not know how to let go. I fear I will fall off a cliff's edge and there will be no one to catch me. My fear paralyzes me and makes me go over and over the same track, unable to try something new.

By again recognizing that I was powerless over my incest perpetrator, I am better able to understand why my inner child is still so vulnerable to paralysis, so unwilling to let go. Yet today I can empower myself to act on my own behalf. I do not need to go round and round with futility. Sometimes I must sit with the discomfort of not knowing what the outcome of a situation will be. I yearn to be able to look around the next corner. I convince myself I could relax if I could see what's coming. But if I try to play God, I cannot have the gift of faith in my higher power.

I choose today to stay with the moment, even when I am uncomfortable. Feeling uncomfortable is a part of being alive. I choose to believe I can be safe even when I don't know what today will bring.

I am grateful to have life today and the opportunity to awaken fully to it.

Growing up in an abusive family was deadening. My heart was rarely open. I was on guard, jumpy, prepared for the next crisis. My attitude became very negative, "Why me? Why do I have *this* instead of *that?*" I came to expect the worst in every situation.

As I heal, those negative attitudes no longer feel like the right garments to wear. I begin to notice all I have to be grateful for: my friends, the honesty of my sister survivors, my home, the opportunity to be healing now in the first generation of incest survivors who have growing support for speaking out and getting on.

When I feel deficient or bereft, composing a gratitude list will lift me. It will not interfere with my ability to see my problems and deprivations, but it will keep the light of gratitude shining.

I validate what I remember and allow it to become part of my total experience.

Incest memories sometimes come back in a dim, hazy form, which makes it difficult for me to be clear about them. I feel I cannot be sure of them until I see them in sharp focus. I fear I might falsely accuse my perpetrator. If only I could see him or her more clearly, I would be able to *know* for certain that this was my experience.

When I am going through the emotional recall of incest, regardless of how clear my visual recall is, I give myself the benefit of the doubt. As a child I may have seen my perpetrator as unreal, ethereal. Perhaps this was the way my psyche protected me. I might never remember my abuser's outlines distinctly. When I honor what I remember as I remember it, I feel whole because of that acceptance. When I am ready to share my memories with a therapist or others in my sexual abuse group, I give my inner child the gift of being heard by receptive ears, and I no longer feel so alone or so unsure.

I am whole and clean and fully entitled to give new life by birthing a child.

Many incest survivors have not had children because, having not worked through the abuse they suffered, they feared they might not be good parents. Many survivors only get in touch with their abuse when their children are born or when their children reach certain ages, perhaps an age at which they were first abused. Some women, because of specific abuse, do just about anything to avoid going to a doctor, particularly a gynecologist.

In recovery we learn that despite our feelings about our body, we are not tainted or tarnished. We have nothing to be ashamed of. The shame attached to the incest never should have rested with us. It is natural for us to have fears about our children, their vulnerability, the possibilities that they might encounter sexual abuse as we did. But as long as we work to become aware and heal ourselves, we pose no threat to them. In fact we have much sensitivity to offer them. Our work in protecting them and teaching them to protect themselves by developing good boundaries can contribute to our healing.

I allow myself the satisfaction of finishing business with others.

One way I have learned to reinforce the notion that I am not entitled to a real and full life is to exit relationships on the run and suffer later in confusion and angst over my losses. My incest experiences signaled the message, "You're not worth full consideration. Dignity is not for you."

To take the opposite stand, to say, "Oh yes it is," may raise the pitch of the voices that speak against me to a cacophonous level. But in recovery I have the voices of my recovering sister survivors to help reinforce my yes. I have a sense of my higher power's will for me.

When relationships come to a point of ending or transition, I can express myself fully. I can appreciate the gifts I've received from others and hear them express what I've given to them. I can share some of my grief over the impending separation. If I listen closely I may understand whatever unfinished business lies between us and take this opportunity to move to completion. When I do so, I heal myself. I show myself I am worthy of full consideration and am settling for nothing less.

Home is where I settle down and feel the strength of developing roots.

I am entitled to belong in a place of my choice. During the sexual abuse, I was misused. This resulted in my feeling misplaced, as if I didn't belong in a place I had thought was mine—home. It was no longer a safe place. I spent as much time away from home as possible.

I no longer live in a danger zone. Yet if I have never taken back "home" the way women in the 1970s took back the night with candlelight marches, vigils, and speeches about rape, I may still be living in my home without allowing myself to settle.

I ritually evict the ghosts of my unsafe childhood home from my present home. I allow myself to root and feel safe and secure. I belong here. I do not need to occupy myself with notions that I should be somewhere else or ready to move at any moment.

I set and accept my limits, and expect them to be accepted by others.

I am a human being among human beings. We each have limits, and setting our limits with others can help us define ourselves. If I cannot say no, how true will my yes be?

It was strongly impressed on me during the incest that I had no right to set a limit or say no, because it was disregarded when I did. When I set a limit, I was shamed out of it by a parent, accused of being stingy or inadequate, or mocked for putting myself ahead of others. These were tactics used by my incestuous family to compensate for the fact that there was no room for individual growth. The survival of the system depended on denial of the childrens' needs.

Today I struggle to set my limits and stand fast behind them. I will not castigate myself if I have equivocated. This is a necessary state of walking through the conflict that is raised in me when I stand for myself first. I will expect progress, not perfection, and give myself credit for the steps as I take them.

I give myself the pleasure of an enthusiastic response; I am worthy of celebration.

A child's sense of self-worth is validated by receiving an enthusiastic response to her being, whether that is a smile meeting her smile, a greeting meeting her arrival, or applause meeting her achievement. Children growing up in abusive environments do not receive this enthusiasm, or if they do they cannot be comfortable with it because it might be a setup for the next devastating incident of abuse or some other form of humiliation.

My ability to respond to enthusiasm and to allow it in myself was damaged in my childhood. Today I still feel anxious if someone applauds me or even meets me directly with a smile. But I choose to identify this anxiety for what it is rather than continue to deprive myself and live as if I can only afford to be blasé about everything. The enthusiasm I give myself helps to heal me. It tells me I am worthwhile. It tells me I am an alive and passionate being.

I create a home in which I can rest freely. I no longer need to keep on the run.

In the home I grew up in, my well-being was threatened. I stayed away from it as much as possible when I was young. I spent a lot of time with another family or sometimes I just stayed outdoors.

Many of us who used this tactic may still have times even now when we do not allow ourselves to rest fully in our home. Though we have created safe and pleasant spaces, we may find ourselves constantly keeping busy and running away from our home. Or we may have put ourselves in a living situation in which we do not feel safe.

It is time in my healing to look at my home life and make sure it is safe and comfortable. Am I letting myself use it as a place of rest and recovery?

*I hold to myself and express my feelings instead
of abandoning myself by stuffing them.*

In my family I learned there was no room for
me to express my feelings or have them accepted.
Feelings were threatening to my family's system.
So I carried the burden of silence and stuffed my
feelings to get them out of the way. While this
saved my feelings from being trampled by others,
it also made me feel bereft and abandoned because I was not able to be myself. I felt stored,
kept whole and alive in some small room inside
myself. In there I was able to preserve my true
self, but I need not stay in that small room any
longer.

When I take a close look, I see that I abandon
myself when I stuff my feelings out of fear that
they will not be acceptable. It is more painful
than ever to do this now because, gratefully, I am
no longer adapted to it. I see the consequences—
how stuffing my feelings takes me away from myself and those I love. It secures me from risk, but
only in a way that closes a door I need to keep
open. Today I want to stay open to my feelings
and choose a particular kind of risk—the risk to
share myself and find myself acceptable after all.

I learned blame as a child as an evasion tactic. Now I learn instead to relate by sharing my feelings.

Blame was attached to just about everything in my family of origin. It was thrown around like a hot potato. I learned to toss it quickly to another or to take it even when it wasn't mine in an effort to gain control. Either way was a mode that blocked deeper relating. Instead of focusing on how family members felt, the communication centered on justifying or defending oneself about each and every interaction. Parents acted like umpires, making calls about where the blame should rest rather than drawing out the children's feelings.

Blame is insidious but not so simple to put down. It can feel as if life will not go on unless I tell that other person how wrong they've been and why they are to blame. Even when I comprehend how unproductive this is, the impulse still holds great power. One incident at a time, I can let go of the need to blame and open to a new way.

In the new way I share my feelings. Rather than saying, "You make me feel hurt," I say, "I am hurting." Rather than saying, "Your changing plans on me is messing up my life," I say, "It's hard for me to have plans change. I'm upset." I am more at home when I own my feelings.

*I build a trusting and healing relationship with
my inner child, attending to her needs daily.*

My inner child is very needy, not because she
is excessively demanding, but because she has
long been neglected. She has learned to protect
herself against hurt by being insular and isolat-
ing. She requires an invitation to come out. She
requires consistently kind treatment to feel safe
enough to share her wants and needs with me.
She needs me to be playful and easygoing with
her. She needs me to be serious and willing
to grieve with her. Sometimes she is enraged and
inarticulate.

Whatever her requirements, I can begin today
to build a relationship with her, being willing to
give her my attention and break the bonds with
my family of origin that mandate ignoring her. I
become aware of her presence and her needs and
try to accept her just as she is, whether shy, re-
clusive, aggressive, or ashamed. I look her in the
eye in the mirror and recognize her. I greet her
and welcome her. This is the beginning of opening myself to know her and love her.

I do not allow anyone to make me feel invisible.
I am visible to myself.

In our family some of us perceived there was much to be gained by being invisible, so we became emotionally or physically absent when possible. Others of us learned to feel invisible when we went to our mother to say, "This is what my stepfather did to me," and were met with the stony silence of denial, or her response, "No, he wouldn't do that," or some other statement that implied there was something wrong with us, not him.

To begin healing we need to find compassion in ourselves for that child who suffered the deprivation of invisibility and the fears of being visible. We need to let her know we understand why she needed these defenses.

I begin restoring my right relationship to visibility by becoming visible to myself. When someone ignores me, I realize that someone ignored me, not that I was not present or deserved to be ignored. When someone wants to put me up on a pedestal, I decline the invitation. I do not want to gain my visibility by being a performer but by being simply me.

*When I look with compassion at my tendency
to procrastinate, I experience my fear of finishing things.*

It is important for me to finish things. Yet my
desire to finish some things is continually
thwarted by self-sabotaging impulses that keep
me from my goal. I may start a new project, run
myself down and get sick, or lose my concentration or interest in a project that needs finishing.
When this happens, it will not help to chastise
myself or cut down the efforts I have already
made.

As an incest survivor, I have always been torn
between craving recognition and visibility and
trying to feel safe by being invisible. Finishing
projects, accumulating achievements—these
make me visible. They show I am committed to
the belief that I count. This message, antithetical
to the message of my incest, may raise up the
voices in me that say, "Don't you dare. I'll get you
for this."

Today I can follow my blueprint for change by
letting in new messages. By sticking to simple
slogans like First Things First, I will complete
things. My awareness of the voices in me can
help me remember my wounds so I treat myself
carefully in the process. They will not stop me
unless I choose to let them.

It behooves me to discriminate between past and present, between facts and feelings, and I am learning to practice this.

Most of my life I've spent overwhelmed by my past and by my feelings. Often when I thought I was in the present, I was pulling a wagonload of baggage without being aware of how it dragged behind me. I was not conscious of how much my feelings about the past were coloring my present perception of reality.

As I consciously approach the influence the abuse had on me, I become more able to make distinctions. For instance, if someone steps on a seedling in my garden, crushing it, and I become enraged, I can separate my anger at the person's mistake from my deep rage that comes from my feelings of being crushed as a child.

Today I exercise my powers of discernment. When I become overwhelmed by my feelings, I slow down and sift through them. I do not jump to the conclusion that my feelings represent the facts, but neither do I ignore them or push them away.

I ask for the guidance to stay in the present with my losses.

As incest survivors many of us suffered what seemed like more than our fair share of childhood loss. We lost the ability to trust someone who may have been of great importance to us. We lost our innocence and the ability to play with ease. We lost the sense of autonomy about our body.

In my present life I encounter losses. Loved ones die. Relationships end or change because I move or others move away from me, physically or emotionally. Even when I let go of old ways of being, I encounter losses. There is nothing wrong with me for feeling sad with my losses. I no longer need to hold the sadness away from me. But neither do I need to reencounter all my old losses as I've often done in the past. For this will overwhelm me.

When a present loss brings up echoes of all my other losses, I will ask my higher power to help me stay in the now. I can handle my current losses with the tools I have been given. I do not need to feel victimized. Everyone sustains losses. I have not been singled out.

I am free to use the full range and power of my imagination for the purposes I desire.

My imagination is a part of my spirit. In my incest experience, I learned to use it to protect me, to take me away from a situation that was too painful to feel. I used it to create a mythology for my family that seemed to permit me some dignity. I became agile at using my imagination to create fantasies of alternative worlds—worlds that could nurture me.

As I recover, I become more and more interested in living in reality. I realize my fantasy excursions have served me well, but they have also isolated me. Today I use my imagination for other purposes. While its development flourished to soothe my wounds, it does not have to be used up in the healing. I can unfetter my imagination and allow it to help me envision the person I want to be. I can allow it to amuse me and encourage my ability to be playful and original. I can free myself to use it in any way I desire.

Working with obsessive energy burns me out.
I will slow down to take care of my most
immediate needs.

When hungry, eat; when tired, rest; when lonely, call a friend. These balanced solutions seem too simple for many of us. We tend to go for more of everything rather than slow down to experience the satisfaction of enough is enough. When work is involved, it is especially easy to be seduced into producing compulsively if we get reinforcement for doing our job well. But our energy bank is likely to reject withdrawals after a time if we neglect our spirits.

Overrunning our own needs feels no better than being overrun by others. Even when we are working hard, even when others are counting on us, we still have many aspects of our life to nurture. As we learn to take care of ourselves more lovingly, we will feel more valued. Whether our work involves taking care of others, building houses, or putting data into a computer, we will feel less fatigued at the end of a day if we simply let ourselves be at the same time as we perform and do.

I am entitled to lay out my boundaries in a way that will grant me spaciousness both within and without.

In my incest experiences I got the message, "Move over. You're not entitled to stand your own ground" when someone else's needs were contrary to my own. My child may have cried out, "Not fair, not fair!" Nevertheless, I had to relinquish my space for my own preservation.

Today as an adult I have the capacity to heal from this. I need not cower or move aside because someone commands me to with authority. I can stand and fight back. I can state my case clearly and let the intruder know he or she is overstepping my boundaries. I do not need to move them an inch to suit his or her purposes. I will instead put my energy into seeking and finding the guidance I need to determine my rights in the situation. Whether it be to acquire legal assistance or to share my fears with fellow incest survivors, I will take care of myself. Each time I stand up for myself, I will note the contribution I have made to my growing self-esteem. I am building a new foundation. I am granting myself the spaciousness that I was deprived.

Making for myself or wearing a mandala can help remind me I am drawn to inner wholeness.

Mandala is a Hindu word for magic circle, which Jung used as a symbolic representation of the human psyche. The Navaho use the mandala as a pattern for sand paintings, which are made to bring a person who is ill back into harmony with herself and the cosmos—in other words into health.

We who have been deeply wounded as children need to create individual rituals and symbols for our healing. We may also use the collective healing power we discover in the universe. Many of us have had dreams that gave us a clue to our wellness, perhaps after a series of painful nightmares. There might have been a sun in our dream, or a moon. A round meadow, a pendant. Or we might dream up our own symbol now, in wakeful contemplation.

I hold my mandala in my mind's eye when I feel fragmented. The way I am drawn to its power is my attraction to my wholeness.

*I learn to give freely without being bound by
the expectation of a return.*

Because my rights were not respected as a
child, because I was robbed of my natural boundaries, I feel afraid to give to others now. I fear my
openness and generosity will be exploited. I fear
if I open my armor to give, something may come
through to injure me. But if I live by this fear, I
deprive myself.

In my recovery group I can safely explore my
capacity to give—by serving as a leader, offering
a hug, or listening to someone in pain. I can
touch another's pain simply by listening to it. I
do not need to do anything about it.

I can also reach out to my loved ones, bringing
the same principles I learn in recovery to them. I
experience my generosity as a gift from my higher
power. I let go of temptations to attach strings to
it or wishes to be rewarded.

I seek guides to help me build bridges to new ways of trusting.

Trust is a feeling of comfort and security that develops in me over time as I share myself and receive a caring, concerned, and nonjudgmental reaction. I need a repeated series of these responses for trust to build. I will set myself up for failure if I demand perfection, but I can learn to take note of consistency.

It seems quite natural that I have had difficulty with trust in the past, since its development was not fostered in my childhood. Those I entrusted myself to sporadically abandoned, abused, or neglected me. Since I had to depend on them for my essential needs, I had to go on "trusting" them, but with a twist in my gut that told me all was not well. I will need to follow other models to learn a new system.

The guides who help me build bridges may be therapists or people in my incest survivor's group. We entrust each other around the common cause of improving our safety and well-being.

*I steer clear of negativity, understanding that
my problems all have meaning.*

When problems come up, I do not need to feel
discouraged. To be disappointed or discouraged
may be my first reaction because I had no means
of coping with problems as a child, except to
abandon my true self and adopt a false front.
Thus each time a problem presented itself, I felt
revictimized.

Today I have a new blueprint to work with,
new tools and coping skills. I stay close to my
true self and evaluate the problems in light of my
needs and desires. If I experience inner conflict, I
try having a dialogue with my inner child who
can often tell me more about my feelings and the
fears she is holding.

I see my problems as hills to be ascended on my
journey. They often make me strain and stretch myself in the exercise they provide me. But as time
passes, they hold less power to provoke thoughts of
hopelessness and despair. I trust I will see their
meaning further down the road.

If I establish and remain faithful to my boundaries, I will be safe from engulfment.

I have a great fear of engulfment, derived from real experiences in my past. This fear plays a prominent role in my relationships, especially as they become more intimate. It is possible for me to feel quite positive that another person wants to take me over for his or her own purposes and has no interest in me as an individual, even when this is not so. How can I find my way out when I feel trapped in the maze of this confusion?

I can recognize I am in a flashback to my childhood and the feelings I experienced then. Even if I cannot draw myself out of the flashback, it helps to be aware that I am in one. I can realize that my boundaries in reality remain unbroken. They envelop and contain me. I can visualize my boundaries like an invisible shield that wards off forces that would engulf me, and know that I am safe from them.

I comfort my inner child by visualizing her sitting on my lap while I tell her things she needs to hear.

All children require comforting to settle down with a sense of well-being. I did not receive this in my family of origin. Instead, I learned ways of comforting myself that took me away from others, such as rocking myself, or relating to toys or animals as safe company.

When my inner child is upset now, she tends to take over and make me feel inadequate and small. I can take this as a sign of her need for comfort and visualize a scene in which I parent her. I bring her out, sit her on my lap, and ask her what she needs a mother to say to her. "Tell me I wasn't to blame. No matter how vulnerable and pathetic I look, I didn't make the bad stuff happen. I didn't bring it on me," she says. I tell her that's true. She was not to blame. I tell her I'm taking care of her now. I'm strong enough to protect her. I can't guarantee that I am always 100 percent consistent because that's unrealistic, but I am doing the best I can at all times to be there for her.

I visualize her going back inside me to again become a part of me. I visualize my inner child and my adult aligned with each other.

September

I seek to find places where there are people who can hear my pain.

Pain shared seems to have its power reduced by about half. I need to remember this when my pain grows large and feels unbearable.

To go through incest recovery, I must return to events that were very painful and that threatened me greatly. I may have gone through them numbly as a child. I will never have to go through them again, but I may have to encounter the horror and pain that I stored then and have never fully felt.

I need support to do this. I seek to be in the places where I can find such support from a therapist, an incest survivor's group, or trustworthy friends. I give myself the gift of sharing, even when I am at my lowest moments. In sharing I become unburdened. I can then continue my journey.

I will deepen myself by grieving my losses.

Because a person in my family who had power over me betrayed me, it was necessary for me to create a fantasy image of my family. I did this to cover for the perpetrator and to provide some security for myself by avoiding the true picture of what I had encountered. My way of modifying the truth and the fantasy picture I created will have to be given up in my recovery. As I release it I grieve—for the early loss of my innocence, for the lack of a trustworthy power in my childhood, and even for the loss of this old cover that lent me the illusion of security.

Sometimes grief grows directly out of the recovery process; sometimes it is provoked by the death of a loved one or another loss, such as the loss of a job or the end of a close relationship. The feeling of grief, unrecognized, can frighten and throw me. I fear if I look inside I will find emptiness. Thus, I long to get out of myself. But when I am able to sit still, I come to understand my discomfort as meaningful. Some aspect of me is dying; another aspect of me is being born. Grief is the labor before delivery.

In confronting my perpetrator I right the scale of loyalty by giving up protecting the other person from their own behavior.

Preparing to confront a perpetrator is a nerve-wracking experience. I use the network I have built by reaching out to others for support as I walk through many stages and feelings. I have long protected my perpetrator from his or her acts by my silence, but I am about to make a break with this relationship that has had great longevity. If the perpetrator is a mother or father, the fear is heightened by the collective thrust of universal messages such as: Honor thy father and mother. How dare I act against the weight of all this?

I honor and acknowledge the truth of my experience by confronting my perpetrator. I offer him or her the opportunity for a relationship based in reality. My act is not done out of spite, but out of my desire to be who I am, give back what belongs to another, and cease to carry anyone's burdens but my own. This is not an act of retaliation, though I may often desire retaliation. This is an act of honoring myself.

For today I will let myself be in the moment and open myself to accepting feelings and circumstances exactly as they are.

Before action I need awareness and acceptance. Often I become aware that something is bothering me and go immediately into action, dizzying myself with activity. This is not truly action. It is resistance. Eventually, I wear down from running around and around, expecting to get somewhere but only spinning like the wheel of a stuck car sinking deeper in the mud. I ask myself why anyone would do such a frustrating thing.

In our incest experiences we may have been unable to take effective action, such as getting away from the perpetrator or telling others and being believed. The best we could do then may have been to blitz it out of sharp focus and bear it.

But today we have a new chance, a new day. I do not need to carry my old defenses forward. I can safely bring myself to each moment of my day and accept and be with it. I can pray for the guidance I need when I am troubled. The right actions will emerge with clarity and even sometimes with ease.

The more I own of my true experience, present and past, the more I am able to know my substance.

Often when we first identify ourselves as survivors of childhood sexual abuse, we are able to come up with a graphic description of the events, yet we may feel a great distance from our feelings. We may know the perpetrator was our brother or our father, for instance, and still be unable to point our finger directly at this person and deliver our anger in his direction. We may focus instead on the lack of protection provided by our mother, or we may simply misdirect a lot of anger at loved ones who are trying to be there for us.

When I know something, yet try to disown it because it feels too uncomfortable to really own it, I only delay my healing. I suffer from internal conflict. I am likely to wrongly direct my anger or conflict onto people or events around me, pushing them away. I cannot move forward if I have half my weight on one foot and half on the other. I need to stop, accept what is mine, and trust I will be given the guidance to work through it.

When I triumph over forces that have held me down in the past, I will allow myself to feel free and joyful.

It is important for me to live in the moment always, including in my moments of victory. I have worked hard to create fertile ground for healthy growth to occur. There will be moments when I can see signs of this healthy growth—I may be offered a job I wanted, fall in love, or simply stand up for myself in a situation I formerly would not have had the courage to stand up in. At these moments I need to recognize my achievements, be joyful, and allow them to become part of who I am.

Because of the shame and low self-esteem resulting from the abuse I received, it may be difficult to allow myself to feel victorious. I have spent years in the familiar shadows of victimization. When victories came along, I barely allowed myself to acknowledge them. I did not count them as real events and significant moments. Today I feel the spaciousness created by my sincere hard work, and I allow myself to celebrate my successes.

My needs are valid and worthy of attention.

How do I feel when I am needy? Certainly far from relaxed and comfortable. I become afraid to remain in my own skin. Afraid if I ask for my need to be met I will be ignored or rejected, my need trivialized or scorned. Afraid recognizing my need will only lead me back to feeling powerlessness. Isn't it easier to not need anything than to be faced with these risks that come with putting my needs out?

Because being needy is so laden with extra baggage and tension for me, I am apt to see my need negatively even before I lay it out for anyone to see. I can work with that by reminding myself my needs are valid and worthy of attention. They are part of being human. I tried to push them away because when I was a child they were not respected and validated. But they have never gone away. They will always push through in one form or another. My conscious expression of them grants me a much better chance of having them met.

*No matter how great or small I think are the
strides I have made in my recovery, they are
made apparent and validated each time I pass
my hope on to others.*

Incest survivors' experiences, and the gigantic
long-term effects of those experiences, have long
been denied and silenced in our culture, even in
psychological circles. Few hands were there to
reach out to us. Even when we found the courage
to speak, we might have met with an antagonistic
response. Still, we are fortunate to be living now in
a time when large numbers of incest survivors are
speaking up and documenting their experiences.

As I benefit from being heard by others, I begin
to recognize my responsibility to share my experience and hope with those who are even newer
to breaking silence than I am. I will receive the
gift of hearing my own hope spoken aloud. To
others I will give the gift of connection, of knowing we do not have to do this alone. I will be part
of the growing volume of voices that may save
some child in the future from being abused.

I am entitled to lead a wholesome and satisfying life.

Because my basic sanctity was not honored in my incestuous family, my sense of deserving a life apart from them was given no credence. I was punished repeatedly when I acted in my own interests. Those who I thought loved me looked on me only as an object to satisfy their purposes. How then was I to develop a sense of deserving to lead my own life?

Today I realize that while I was born into my biological family, I need not derive my sense of purpose from the poverty of the messages I was given there. I am a child of my higher power. My spirit has been given a life as rich as that given to any other person. I am no longer dependent on my parents for any sort of sustenance, and I am free to cease to see myself through their eyes. When I look through my own eyes and allow my higher power to shine within me, I see that I can live a satisfying life. My purpose on this planet is to work toward wholeness.

With the help of my sister survivors, I have the courage to choose my direction today and follow it.

Life presents us with a series of crossroads. We must choose again and again to remain on course. We summon up the courage to say yes for ourselves: Yes, I am going to get out from under the effects of this incest. Yes, I am ready to stop beating up on myself. Yes, I want to change careers and I can do it. Then we are momentarily blissed out because our yes has been accepted and we are likely to take up the illusion that nothing can ever go wrong because the Goddess is with us.

But inevitably we are presented with trials, just as in the fairy tales where the prince or knight must pass tests. As women, we have fewer role models of how to overcome trials in our life. We are relegated in fairy tales to the passive role. We are the prize the prince is acting for. Yet our life does contain trials. Our decisions will be challenged and we will have to choose to say yes again at each crossroad.

I learn to resolve conflict within by repeatedly saying yes against the still lively voices inside that protest. Each time I do, they lose power. When I feel defeat, I reach to those recovering with me and receive strength from their courage.

Today I make necessary separations into conscious encounters that help to define me.

My boundaries were broken early in life, and my incestuous family functioned by continually blurring boundaries. The message this gave me was that I was not separate and entitled to my autonomy. I was offered no lessons in how to balance my individual needs with needs of the family.

Separation has always been a source of pain for me. When I've moved, I've been reluctant to share with friends that real change is about to take place. I've feared they would value me less if I let them know I was leaving. I've feared my feelings of sadness and loss would hurt me more if I brought them out into the light of day instead of pretending I wasn't really feeling them. But my hiding has hurt me more than anything else. It has made me feel invisible, apart from the changes as they occur in my life.

Today I know I am entitled to show up and share my experience truthfully. When I do so, I find acceptance and love for myself.

I ask my higher power for guidance in how to cease committing acts that are destructive to me.

Many of us have self-mutilating habits or behaviors ranging from chewing our nails or our lips to pulling out our hair or cutting ourselves with razor blades. Many of us have attempted suicide. Or we mutilate ourselves on another level by sabotaging any achievement or happiness we have worked for.

As I begin to heal I see how necessary it is to become free of these behaviors. I recognize that in acts of self-destruction I may have been trying to injure the perpetrator who I felt had implanted himself inside me. If I cut myself and spilled my blood, was it not the poisoned blood I was trying to get out of me? As incest survivors we have a deep sense of having had the core of ourselves penetrated, regardless of whether we endured actual sexual penetration.

My blood is clean. I am only me. I need to release the old images that have tortured me. I need the guidance of my higher power to lead me and fill myself anew.

I will first learn to trust my own instincts and then risk trusting others who have proved themselves reliable.

I trusted people in my childhood who betrayed and invaded me. I was wounded by the fact that there was no acknowledgment of this; rather, it was denied and made secret. If my response was rage, this too had to be hidden. From then on there was always a false bottom in my trust system. I reacted in extreme ways, either making myself vulnerable to injury by being overly trusting of others, or finding myself lonely as the result of trusting no one.

Today I begin anew to develop a willingness to trust in a way that first and foremost takes *me* into account. I trust my feelings are present to protect me, but I need to explore them rather than use them to jump to conclusions. In an intimate situation it will feel risky to trust another. Yet I can do so. I can hold and reassure the frightened child within me that I am keeping my eyes open and will continue to express myself. I can detach and hold to my own opinion when someone close seems to want to control me. I can move in and out of complete trust of another, counting on my instincts to guide me wisely.

*I embrace my passion; it is a deep expression of
my self without the censorship of inhibitions.*

During our childhood years we learned to tuck
away our deepest, most passionate feelings because we had virtually no channels through
which to express them. We may have felt passionate within, fiery with rage and malcontent.
We may have had grandiose fantasies of how we
would finally express ourselves. We may have developed an addiction to drugs that muted and
depressed our relationship to our passion while
at the same time deluding ourselves into believing we were expressing it.

As we heal from our abuse and accumulate
more sober and abstinent time from old escapes,
our passion grows stronger. We go through our
rage, finding appropriate places to express it. We
feel how our passion is lodged in us. It was never
safe to express it before, but it is now.

The more I heal, the more my passion flowers.
It is love without bindings. It is the desire for my
whole self to open and emerge.

My path is to correct the distorted perceptions I acquired in the past.

As a child when I perceived one thing to be the truth, I was often told, "No, what your father says is the truth regardless of whether it makes sense or not." I learned to go against my intuition. I learned to gain my perceptions by second-guessing others. Sometimes I tried to keep double track of things—my perception and someone else's perception at the same time. Sometimes it only seemed possible to abandon mine and worry about staying aligned with theirs.

Today, as I heal, I consciously practice validating my own perceptions. I am willing to hear someone else's version of reality, but I do not need to adopt it as mine. After years of distortion, it will not be easy to stay with myself consistently at first. I may succeed, then find myself toppled by old habits before I become aware of them. When this happens, I will simply remind myself of my path and return to it without making my error an opportunity for self-castigation.

Today I am grateful for my ability to change, even though I feel uncomfortable with the feelings that come with new ways.

Change means letting go of the old and taking up the new. It means closing doors that kept me in the past and opening the doors of my present reality.

My incest experience caused me to become rigid in an effort to cling to some narrow perception of my world that allowed me to feel safe. The notion of holding things still, not allowing them to change, offered me a scrap of security. But the nature of life is cyclical and moving. We are all passing through on a journey. Anything we own has really only been temporarily placed in our care by the Great Mother.

When I let go of the old and make room for the new, I expect that my reward will be ease and comfort. Instead I find myself fearful of beginning again and, like a young, tender baby, I need much care and attention to grow and flourish. With time and compassion I will become more comfortable. I give myself this time and compassion.

Through a difficult night I grapple with ghosts, knowing with certainty that daybreak always comes.

Many of us are plagued with sleeping problems, fear of the dark, nightmares, apprehension about having our space invaded. These are problems derived from the reality of our childhood, from incidents in which we were not able to keep ourselves safe and were subject to invasion or frightening treatment.

When I have difficult nights in which I feel as unsafe as I felt as a child, it helps me to detach a little and realize I am in a flashback. My unconscious mind often delivers its messages and memories in sleep through dreams. If I am not ready right away to deal with them, then I can let them roll by, and they will come up to give me another chance in the future. When they frighten me and I feel in limbo with the dark, I hold to the thought that this too shall pass.

At daybreak I receive hope. I watch the dawn and am grateful for a new day. I need only face what is in today. I allow my hope to soar with the rising light of day.

I will take as much time as I need for reflection, allowing myself to let insights dawn and settle to create new perspectives.

Once I admit how wounded I was by the incest and recognize how its effects carried into and profoundly influenced my life, I have an urge to do all the work immediately that would lead me to rise like a phoenix from the ashes. I begin to work relentlessly on dredging up my memories. I feel as if I must become vigilant about standing up for myself at every possible opportunity. It is easy to adopt a purge mentality about how I need to get all this stuff out of me immediately, if not sooner.

But the solution may not be to lock horns so directly with the problem. Healing requires balance. Lessons in standing up for myself can be balanced with lessons in giving myself time for rest and reflection. I need to acknowledge that my wounds will stay with me, and while the pain they cause will change as I give them care and attention, they will still remain a part of me.

I can work in my life today to avoid revictimization. I can begin living in a way that is positive for me without dredging up everything at once. I can periodically take inventory of what I've learned about my incest and let it sit on a shelf awhile until I gain new perspective. This is not denial but a conscious choice to take a break and give my healing time.

I open a window to the consciousness of what gives me pleasure.

My mind is so much more familiar with negative thoughts than with the awareness of what gives me pleasure. I may, in fact, be deriving pleasure from many sources but rarely allowing myself to focus on them.

Today I will take the time to write down a list of all the things that come to mind that give me pleasure. It might look something like this:

The morning sun in my bedroom; forsythia in bloom; the smell of earth; my cat nuzzling her head into my chin; the sound of the mail carrier pulling away from my mailbox; folding up clean laundry; running in new running shoes; tea with someone I cherish; the phone ringing at a lonely hour; creative energy that feels sexual; Mozart.

Noticing how quickly and surely these items spring to my list, I realize I have been enjoying them but as if through a screen that diminished my full appreciation. I allow them now to take a vibrant place on the palette of my day.

I trust relationships are given to me in part to help me see myself. When they become painful, I must turn my attention to see what lesson is present.

I choose my relationships today, yet I do not always understand what they can teach me about myself. When they cause pain or turbulence, I want to throw them out. I fear they are going to hurt me.

My childhood incest experiences robbed me of the freedom to connect with my true nature and distorted my sense of relationships. I felt that to relate meant to be subjugated and overridden.

As I gain maturity, I see that relationships present me with opportunities to grow. Intimate relationships especially provoke me to feel the old feelings, but today's challenge is to realize that I am not being subjugated. I am free to speak openly and stand up so my needs are respected. I have an opportunity to see how two people can function in tandem without either being obliterated. I may require a lot of guidance to have a harmonious relationship, but today I know where to seek out the help that can provide that guidance.

*As the seasons change I witness the cyclical
flow of nature and allow it to reverberate in me.*

In my past I always wanted to slow things
down. Because of the deep insecurity in my
home, I clutched to almost any aspect of life,
wishing to hold it still and derive comfort from
its consistency. As summer turned to fall, I
wished I could stop time or turn it backwards
and hold on to summer a little longer. I loved the
seasons with all their variations, yet resisted the
continuous march from one into another.

Today I see that much of my energy has been
squandered in trying to control things that are
not mine to control. If I stay in the moment with
the changing seasons, I can learn from nature's
demonstration of cyclical growth. Autumn is a
time for some plants and some animals to die.
Then there is dormancy before budding new
birth, followed by a flourishing. I, too, have my
seasons. I do not need to be afraid of any of them.

I take the quiet time I need each day to nourish my intuition and my desire for a peaceful mind.

Sara Orne Jewett, mentor to Willa Cather, wrote to Willa in a letter: "A quiet hour is worth more to you than anything you can do in it." This can be a hard lesson for many of us to learn. We may have used keeping overly busy as a way to avoid our feelings. It may feel very frightening for us to be faced with free, unstructured time. Yet we crave peace. We crave ways to value our being rather than just the doer in us. And we cannot explore deeply inside ourselves if we are not willing to take the risk of becoming quiet.

When I am quiet, I hear my inner guide. I hear the birds sing and sense the harmony of nature. I feel the life force within me. I know I am more than my mind or my body. I am cradled by the universe.

Today I can recognize sadness in myself and express it without negativity.

Feelings of sadness are not eliminated by recovery; in fact, they become more acute for those of us who previously used drugs to avoid them and succeeded in holding them temporarily at bay. Sadness can be related to something specific, such as the anniversary of the death of a loved one, or the recent death of a loved one, or it can be vague and seem to be unattached to any one event. Sadness can trigger my memories of incest, of the ways my inner child had to disappear or split off to protect herself. These memories remind me of my past loss of self.

Today I give vent to my sadness as it enters my day. I will let myself recognize it, perhaps by crying, perhaps by reaching out to share it with a friend. I no longer need to become negative to prove I have reason to feel sorry for myself. That is an old pathway of self-justification that led me to create crises to fit my feelings. Today I can feel compassion for myself in sadness rather than pity. Today I can experience my feelings and let them pass through.

When I feel the blahs, I stay with the feelings and let whatever is lurking beneath the surface come through.

There are different levels of depression—some of them require treatment—but if I am simply having a day of the blahs, what can I do about it? Pay attention to myself despite the way the mood tells me to ignore me. Check myself out for anger, loss, sadness, or possibly all three.

As children we were often ignored or given attention in a way that was hurtful. It would have been impossibly devastating to keep a sharp focus on all that was happening, so we blurred out. Today this may still be part of our feelings of depression, an old familiar way of blotting out pain. Boredom is a clue. If we feel bored, we have probably either gotten mired in the past or are keeping busy predicting the future.

When I sit still with the flat feeling of my depression, I discover I have gotten back under someone's boot, at least inside my mind. My cells feel flattened, oppressed. I hold myself, cry, and let myself know it is okay to feel this and also know I am free to get out from under by taking good care of myself. I do not have to let my mood get worse before I pay attention.

I approve of my being, my willingness, and my growth. I do not need to pander to the approval of others.

As a child I was taught to pay undue attention to how others responded to me. I was given the impression love would be withheld if I were not compliant. Yet when I complied, I received not love but abuse. I was only approved of as an object. I was set up to try harder and harder, but for what? To attain the unattainable?

In recovery I am free to escape this pattern. I use new blueprints I have learned to seek out who I am and to follow a path that helps me remember I have a relationship with a power greater than myself. I make an inventory of my shortcomings and share it with another. I make amends to all I have harmed, including myself. I adopt a way of life in which I will be able to keep an orderly relationship with myself and others one day at a time and share my experience generously. Working at this approach honestly allows me to approve of myself and to detach from others' points of view. I need only be who I am.

Today I have the willingness to release myself from the past and give myself the gift of comprehending all that exists in my present.

I am tired of being mired in the past, running my every experience through the old damaged notions that seemed to have gotten stamped on every cell in my body. I am tired of using misinformation as if it was truth and recreating over and over for myself the same result. I am tired to the bone and yet when I try to escape this alone, I sense my efforts are useless.

I believe that a power greater than myself can release me from the bondage of my past. I ask this higher power to help me now find the truth of my present. It feels unfamiliar to stop the movie of my past from running in the background and encounter silence in its place. But I practice learning to sit still with the quiet. Gradually, I awaken to what is here in my present. I let myself know it is enough. I am well when I let myself be.

I am a child of God; the source of love runs through me.

When I feel low and unlovable, I easily lapse into a sense of shame and worthlessness—the same view of myself I adopted to try to comprehend why the incest was happening to me. It damages me to live with this point of view, for it makes me vulnerable to being revictimized. Finding myself under this heap of punishment, I become resentful because I know I do not deserve this treatment. Justifying myself with resentment, I may then strike out, injuring myself and others, only escalating the damage.

One way for me to exit from this condition is to realize that I am a child of God. When I bury myself under shame, I disregard God's purpose for me—I close the door on my higher power when I am most in need of opening it. It is frightening to trust a power outside of myself when I am feeling vulnerable, but gradually I will learn to do so. I will differentiate between this and the betrayals of trust I encountered in my past. I will allow myself to step outside my shame to love myself at my darkest hour.

As I enter new relationships, I will try to name what I want from them.

In the past I was thrust into a relationship not of my choosing. I was a powerless victim in this relationship, assigned the passive role. I absorbed blame and shame for it, though it was not of my making.

Even away from my family I have recreated some of these dynamics in my relationships: being chosen rather than allowing myself to seek out those who attract me; feeling prey to what others want of me; being ashamed when things go wrong; feeling hopeless about meeting my needs; sexualizing a situation regardless of whether sex is appropriate or desired.

Today I can practice behaving in new ways. I can make a checklist of some sort to keep myself on track. As I begin a relationship, I might ask myself to list three things I'd like to have in it. In a new friendship my list might include honesty, fun, warmth. With a new boss it might be respect, accurate appraisal, clear boundaries. This will show my willingness to actively participate in making my relationships what I want them to be.

I take responsibility for making choices that will allow me to have pleasure and joy in my life.

For many years, both in childhood and in adulthood, it did not seem possible for me to be in charge of my life. In my childhood years I was subject to the will of another; in adulthood this feeling of subjugation recurred even though there was no one standing over me. But because there was so much familiarity to the belief, I acted as if it were true that I was meant to be passive.

As I recover and discover myself, I realize I may often need to stop and ask myself the question, "Am I acting to lead the life I want? Or am I acting as if my purpose is to take care of someone else's needs instead of my own?" If I am not leading the life I would like to, then I am responsible for making the decisions that will let me move closer to myself and my desires. I do not need to rush into hasty decisions, but I do need to realize that I am capable of initiating action.

When I do not feel ready to act, I ask for the guidance of my higher power to gain the understanding I need. I do not ever need to feel I am alone.

*When I recognize that my will is riotously out
of hand in an attempt to be in control, I will
humble myself, put my ego aside, and get out of
my own light.*

I once clung tenaciously to my will as the only
thing that could give me security. I thought, "If
only I could get everything right. . . . If only everyone would behave as I would like them to.
. . . If only I were in charge." But the security I
derived was never more than an illusion. And my
desire to be in charge was never more than a reaction to the way I had been powerless in the incest experience.

Today I know that true security comes from
living in harmony with myself and seeking to be
aligned with the will of my higher power. I must
repeatedly let go of calling on my will to take
charge and instead tap into the spiritual well that
puts me in union with my higher power. I trust
all will be revealed to me as I need to see it. I trust
I will be safe if I humble myself with the belief
that I can only see a small piece of the greater picture at any one time. I need not be ashamed of
this limitation, but concern myself with accepting it as a feature of my humanity.

October

I am filled with truth at my center where I once held shame.

If I look at how I reacted to traumatic events in my childhood, I see that my most common responses were fear and shame. Lessons in responsibility were absent and I was often blamed unjustly. During feelings of shame, I wanted to disappear. I felt embarrassed and unworthy. I protected myself by silence, by stuffing my feelings and keeping out of the way.

As I heal I discover that I have used these responses for protection repeatedly throughout my adult life, and they have served me no better in later years than they did in the early ones. I choose to let go of them and find replacements—new ways that empower me. I break silences rather than keep them. I take my power of speech rather than turn it over to someone else. Each time I practice my new way, I experience some anxiety, but I also note the success I feel when I have been heard. An even greater reward is noticing the warm heart in my center, the place that once shriveled with shame.

Joy lurks in me behind a curtain, ready to leap out whenever I let it.

Even when I feel as if I am in a deep dungeon of darkness, joy is present, only out of my sight.

My incest experiences and my lack of acknowledgment of their painful consequences made me feel joyless. Because of this I felt the need to block all pleasurable impulses. I believed that to let any joy through would be to join others in ignoring my pain.

Today I recognize that all-or-nothing thinking is not necessary for me to maintain my integrity. I have been given joy as a gift and I do not need to deny myself its experience and expression. Instead I can recognize it as a feeling with the potential to heal me. It can come even in the midst of pain. It can shine a ray of light on my darkness and lighten my heart when I feel too heavy to go on. It can be a simple connection that assures me I am coming to know my true nature.

When I honor the right distance for me and take the space I need, I find myself capable of intimacy.

Because my boundaries were so often transgressed in childhood, I did not learn to respect my need to keep them intact. If someone wanted something from me, they were free to move right in. I felt guilty any time I tried to put up a hand and say: "Wait, this is not the right time for me." I was repeatedly revictimized because of my inability to call for the emotional space I needed.

In my relationships today I am regularly presented with the challenge of conflicting needs. When my partner or friends need attachment when I need some distance, I must learn to put myself first a good part of the time. When I go along with their needs instead, I only contaminate the flow of caring with resentment.

I recognize my legitimate need to stay close to myself and my mood and tell others openly when I need distance. When I have respected my boundaries, I will be capable of connecting with others in a good-spirited way.

In spite of possible impediments, I envision what I want and encourage myself to go for it.

It is okay to envision what I want for myself, even if there are problems that may interfere with moving toward that goal. Too often I have stopped before I started because of a negative attitude that told me not to bother, that I wasn't worth it. It was simpler to say, "There will be too many obstacles." . . . "I won't be able to afford it." . . . "I won't be chosen." . . . "Why should I apply and be rejected?" than to look inside and see that I was letting the ghost of defeatism guide me.

When I let my desires through and follow them up with action, I may find that hidden feelings about my abuse come out too. I have to grapple with my fear of taking the active rather than the passive attitude. In my childhood I did not have this choice, but today I can choose to be active.

I will take one action at a time toward my goal, then deal with feelings or problems that arise from that action. When I am ready I will move consciously to the next action. Some of the problems will fall to the side, others will present themselves at the forefront to be taken care of. Even if I am unable to attain my goal completely, I will have accomplished a great deal in having believed in my worthiness to proceed and not be stymied.

As I heal from the abuse I suffered, I become part of the solution by speaking out and acting against abuse wherever it appears in my community.

Many of us engaged now in this healing process would have gone to our graves with our wounds untended had we been born a generation before when even deeper silence about sexual abuse existed. Much as we have suffered, we must consider it a gift and a privilege to be present in this time. The truest means to show we have received this gift is to give it to someone else, thus spreading the awakening.

I share what I have learned about recovery from sexual abuse with others. I participate in helping new groups for sexual abuse survivors get started. I let survivors who are just beginning recovery know that I am available if they need someone to talk to. If I see or know of situations in which children are being abused today, I report it to the appropriate authorities.

I do not consider myself healed but healing. My healing is always enhanced when I share it with others.

*I acknowledge my rage and set about the task
of learning to release it without injuring myself
or others.*

My response to being abused was rage. I had to
bury this rage to survive and it took me many
years to uncover it. I felt it for others—for my
friends, for children, for groups of oppressed
people. While I got some relief from this indirect
expression of my rage, it did not satisfy my inner
child, whose voice I refused to hear crying out
WHY ME? with rage.

In recovery I begin to listen to her. I allow her
to express herself. I give her permission to beat
on the bed, kick and scream, and cry out. Sometimes it feels as if she will only be satisfied if I let
her take over my life. She wants retribution. She
wants to strike out and punish someone for the
injuries that were done to her.

This is where I need to tap the strength of my
higher power to bring to my inner child a feeling
of care and concern. I need to show her compassion and make a promise to protect her, without
giving in to her desire to be in command of my
life. For if I strike out carelessly with her rage, I
may hurt loved ones, including myself.

Today when my emotions become heated, I can choose to practice self-restraint, distinguishing between this and stuffing my feelings.

My response to my childhood traumas was to stuff my feelings. I learned quickly this was best when I attempted to express myself and was met with severe threat or disregard.

As I come into my own in recovery, I rediscover my ability to differentiate and comprehend what I am feeling. I feel like a first grader as I express my feelings, for I have never enjoyed much experience in this area. I easily go out of balance with emotions like anger or rage and suddenly find myself on a tear with my expression. If I am trying to express old business along with current business, I may damage myself and my relationships. While a tantrum may relieve me of built-up pressure, it will not solve my problems. I need to look inward and assess if I have properly directed my feelings.

It will not harm me to step back and practice self-restraint with my feelings. It will not suppress my feelings if I gain distance from them, give them time, share them with an uninvolved friend, or stop to reorient myself with prayer or meditation.

"What ifs" only take me on a detour away from acceptance of what is.

There are many days in which I am plagued by "what ifs" and "if onlys" and am not even able to recognize them as distractions. Surely this was one way I buffered a too devastating reality when I was a child, or a way I created alternative possibilities to keep myself juggling with ambivalence.

Today I realize that I cannot work with my life and my problems until I accept exactly where I am. There are flights of fancy that might make my life seem more appealing, but ultimately I always come down from them to be faced with the constant of reality. To accept what is does not require being depressed about it. It may be difficult to assess the damages honestly and allow myself to feel the places where I have been broken, but it will also be heartening to be filled with my true experience.

When I hear my inner voices saying "What if that hadn't happened? . . ." "If only you had been smart enough not to . . ." I will gently still them. I will not punish myself for their presence or try to banish them permanently. I will simply say good-bye as soon as I notice them.

When I hear my mind having a conversation
with more than one person and no one else is
present, I will simply stop and let it go.

There are voices inside my head that besiege
me with chatter and confuse me. Often their talk
keeps me away from underlying feelings of pain.
These voices began in my childhood, after or during incest-related experiences. They blitzed my
mind so that I would not have to see clearly or
experience the incest so starkly.

I will not have peace of mind unless I let these
voices go. I have spent much of my life trying to
decipher all that they say, feeling I could gain
control by figuring them out. Yet did my figuring
get me anywhere beyond the feeling that I was
scrambling in a cage? Did I ever find out all I
needed to know?

The solution often lies in having the humility
to turn elsewhere for an answer. This might mean
asking for and receiving the guidance of another
person or making conscious contact with my
higher power. I no longer need to do it all alone.

*I emerge from the tunnel of my darkness like
the rising sun at daybreak, growing more
powerful with each passing moment.*

Much of my life has been shrouded in the
gloomy feelings I've carried from my childhood.
Even when I've been highly functional and successful in certain endeavors, I've been frightened
to fully enjoy the success. I've felt like an im-
poster because I was not acknowledging the feelings of my inner child—the dark powerless
moments of being overtaken and abused.

Now as I acknowledge and integrate the feelings of my inner child in recovery, as I validate
her suffering, I find myself emerging. Like the
larva from a cocoon, I move out of my dark tunnel toward the light of day. I fear I will always be
heavy with the weight of knowledge of the abuse
I encountered, yet I discover I am lighter as well
as stronger. My power grows in me like a sun.

*I acknowledge my anger today, honoring its value
in letting me know when I am threatened.*

Anger is an emotion I was taught to repress. Its
value was given only negative significance in my
teachings. If I expressed anger I was treated as if I
were a dangerous person, even potentially in-
sane. If I acted out my anger, I was severely punished for it.

No wonder I do not readily welcome my anger
now as a useful emotion. I fear it instead. Yet I am
learning that it is part of my armature, an important
feeling that can protect me. Just as my earlier beliefs
were acquired—not innate—I can reeducate myself
about the usefulness of my anger, listen to it, evaluate it, and express it appropriately.

I need not rage at someone to have my anger
noticed. I need only own it and keep my expression of it simple. This might mean stepping back
to get a little distance. It might mean stating, "You
just hurt me and I'd like an apology." When I feel
angry but don't know why, if I look inward I will
surely come away with greater understanding.

*I have the capacity to forgive myself when I am
ready to make this choice.*

Many of us have lived with the mistaken as-
sumption that self-forgiveness only fits at the end,
after everything else is done. Perhaps we imagine
ourselves at the very last minute on our deathbed,
allowing in the light of self-forgiveness. Perhaps we
have heard and read of such experiences that reinforce this notion. But because people have such experiences does not mean we cannot choose to have
them at other times.

The best time for self-forgiveness is now. I allow myself to become quiet and meditative. Perhaps what I visualize is my inner child coming
toward me. I notice her posture, the expression
on her face. Is she fearful? Does she ring her
hands in worry? Am I ashamed of her? No. I embrace her. I realize her ways of survival have
brought me to this day. I forgive her. I tell her that
I love her and am grateful for her.

I forgive my adult self also. Whatever I have
wanted to see as transgression or deviation from
my path is actually my path. Every junction is a
good place to realize that and forgive myself for
rejecting myself.

I seek through prayer and meditation to be in contact with the force I call God, and to live in harmony with It.

As an incest survivor, despite some healing, my trust system is fragile. One way it grows stronger is by prayer and meditation.

I am free to choose my own methods of prayer and meditation according to my nature and the images that rise in me when I imagine a higher power. If I want I can use my incest group as a higher power. Or I can picture a higher self like a light shining within me, relate to nature's awesomeness, make a regular practice of yoga or zazen, read spiritual literature, or attend a church service.

Praying for knowledge of God's will and the power to carry it out can help me heal the distortions my incest created about power. In seeking the power to carry out God's will, I become willing to have power in my life—the power that comes from integrity and connection with my spiritual source, not the power of appearing tall because I am stepping on someone else.

I trust I am where I am supposed to be in the process of my life. Instead of looking for solutions in the future, I seek peace and acceptance now on my journey.

All life is fluid. I am always moving through a process. My attempts to arrange things so that I can draw a straight line from the problem to the solution are futile. I create greater pain for myself when I resist the natural flow of life.

Today I make the choice to see myself as part of the design. If my life is moving from crisis to crisis so much that it resembles my family of origin, I can note how I am partaking of that and ask myself why. Is there some consolation in returning to the old mode? Do I need to seek more help to trust where I am in my process? Have I forgotten how much safer I feel when I stay in the now? I can turn my attention to accepting where I am and remember I have the power to make choices.

I look upon the beauty and power of nature with the wonder and innocence of my inner child's eyes.

I've often felt robbed of my wonder and innocence by the need to shut away my exploratory desires to protect myself against harsh realities. If I developed a pattern of protecting myself this way, I do not need to cling to it any longer.

When I visit the ocean or a forest or any place of beauty, I let myself meditate on the innocence of my inner child. I invite myself out to play. I enjoy the water, wind, sand, and sun. It gives me pleasure to feel my wonder. The fact that I remember the injuries that occurred to me in my childhood does not take away the delight I can experience now. I can have my memories and also experience awe and wonder. I have wept for my inner child and rocked her in sorrow. Now I let her also have joy.

I deserve and will give myself the full enjoyment of playing.

My inner child knows how to play, although my relaxation in play has been harshly interrupted by my tension about the incest. Thus, I may associate being playful with an ominous feeling of danger and not simply be able to relax into this aspect of my being. I find vacationing stressful, for it gives me the gift of unstructured time in which to focus only on satisfying my desires.

I will practice allowing my playfulness to come out and be exercised daily. I will allow myself to plan and take vacations, and believe I truly deserve them. I will allow myself to travel to a foreign or unfamiliar land to enjoy the stimulation of difference, rather than fearing my safety is in jeopardy. I will work with my fears one day at a time when they become aroused. And I will walk through each new experience, allowing my inner child the joy of an open, creative imagination.

I will allow myself to experience the healing power of laughter and the balancing effect of play on all the work I have done.

I allow myself to feel excitement over my development.

Watching a baby screech with delight while learning to walk or exploring a new place, my memory is refreshed with the excitement that comes naturally with achievement and development. As I encountered the trauma of abuse while growing up, anxiety obscured that pure sense of excitement. I did not have adequate boundaries or ways to protect myself, nor did I have a reliable protector. Thus, times of excitement often also became times of distress and injury. For example, when I was old enough to travel on public transportation alone, which was exciting, I was not given adequate preparation for warding off molesters. I encountered one and this confused my experience of adventure.

In my adult life when I feel excited, I am often close to panic. Many times I have subverted the event that brought the excitement out of unrecognized fear. This has led to deprivation. I am ready now to make the necessary distinctions so that I can enjoy my excitement and know and embrace my fears.

I look upon the gift of my life as a wondrous journey.

My innocence, the wondrous vision of my childhood, was stolen from me very early. I am fortunate that I was able to retain some of it by returning to it in the safety of aloneness, but this meant my pleasure had to be accompanied by isolation.

It is time now to reclaim wonder and allow myself the gift of its vision. To sit with my friends and listen to a rushing waterfall, to walk in the night and watch the stars, to sit before a crackling camp fire and see the dance of its flames, and to know that I have a relationship with all I see, hear, feel around me. It is a wonder to realize that some old fears I never thought would leave me have passed on. It is a wonder to realize the Great Mother has always provided comfort for me, even when I feared her elements.

As thoughts or feelings of unworthiness arise, I learn to let them float by instead of grasping at them as cues to self-sabotage.

Because I was ill-treated as a child—and so came to believe that I must be inherently unworthy—it is difficult for me to make positive changes without being plagued by inner attacks on myself. When I am offered a good job, or realize there is a loving community available to me, or am able to move into a peaceful home, I hold back. Inner voices grow louder, telling me: "You can't have this. Who do you think you are? Don't trust. These are the kinds of things that come to other people, not you."

In the past I have let these voices set me up for self-sabotage. I would take my cue to prepare for defeat. But as I progress in my healing this no longer suits me. I am finished with defeat. I am willing to feel temporarily uncomfortable as I adjust to the notion that I am worthy, I can open my gates to receive all that comes my way today.

*I will balance my day with enough work, play,
and quiet time to nourish my whole being.*

When there is a major job ahead of me, I
sometimes fall into believing it would be best to
leave all else behind and plow straight ahead
with it. But I will soon find my spirit growing
hungry for other types of food.

Any activity done with a compulsive attitude
soon spins in a circle and takes my energy without giving any back. It puts a fog about me and
blocks me from my feelings. This may be why I
used compulsive behavior in seeking to escape
the pain of incest. Now I recognize and mourn
for the energy it robbed from me.

Today I know that to respect myself and have
dignity as a human being, I need to allow myself
to *be* rather than always *do*. When I find myself
overworking, I will practice reminding myself
that it is okay, even valuable, to stop to redirect
myself to a more balanced life.

*I will cease self-mutilating behaviors whenever
I become aware of them and seek the support
I need to feel my feelings instead.*

As abuse survivors some of us developed self-mutilating behaviors to express our pain. We did these in a compulsive manner to numb ourselves just as we might have used alcohol or other drugs. Even though they have the effect of numbing us, paradoxically these behaviors grew out of the need to create demonstrable evidence that we were injured.

In my healing I make a practice of giving up these behaviors. When I feel the need to do them, I recognize that they have helped me block my deep feelings of powerlessness and the unrecognized pain of my abuse.

Now is the time to permit myself to feel these feelings. Much as it appeals to me to put it off until later, the sooner I give myself the respect and love I deserve by taking in and recognizing my woundedness, the sooner I will begin to heal.

I use writing to help me get in touch with my feelings more clearly.

Thoughts and feelings are forever flashing through our mind or racing around to make us feel as if we are squirrels on a turning wheel. One way to intercept obsessive thinking is by writing down our thoughts. Attending to and documenting our thoughts is likely to take them to a place where we can make better sense of them and where they can become useful.

I will keep a journal for recording things. I do not need to determine exactly what purpose it will serve. I will record my dreams, my hopes and desires, my disappointments, the things that make me angry. I will record my gratitude list. I will record my incest memories and what I learn of how those experiences influenced my life. I will record my milestones of progress.

If I want to look back over my writings periodically, I will use my journal this way. If I never wish to see it again, that is okay too. I am creating this journal not out of "shoulds" but because I want to see if it can help me.

*I humbly enlist the support of my higher power
when I am ready to leave behind old ways.*

Even when I feel entirely ready to let go of old
ways, I feel afraid I will enter a void if I let go
completely. The familiar, even if it is miserable, is
still familiar. Entering new territory requires a
walk in the wilderness of the unfamiliar. As an incest survivor, I am accustomed to being in the
victim role. I have known powerlessness. I have
protected myself with the righteous lot of the injured. To truly change, I must walk out of the
past, out of this role, and take my power.

I will take the time to gradually develop a relationship of trust with my higher power. I do not
trust easily. I must work through the distinction
between humbling myself and being humiliated.
Only when I feel my readiness will I ask God
to remove my shortcomings. Then I will feel a
new freedom and open myself to a new attitude.
I will be amazed at how much I am capable of
changing.

I heal by experiencing the pain of my own abuse. It will never help to abuse others.

Those of us who've been abused sometimes feel as if we're potentially dangerous to others, especially those over whom we have power, such as our children or other children we teach or care for in some way such as baby-sitting. We may feel like powder kegs about to explode, and that a way to release this pressure would be to exploit our power over children in some way that would pay back what was done to us.

When I experience the desire to hurt someone, especially someone I am in a position of power over, I will realize this is an impulse to escape my own pain. It would be irresponsible to act on it and, rather than enhancing my healing, it would set me back. I am an adult now, able to experience impulses without acting on them. I do not need to shame myself for having had the impulse but instead take it as a sign of the need to attend to my pain and then seek to do that.

If I've acted on these impulses and done injury to my children or others in the past, I cease justifying it, own my offenses, and begin making amends. My amends include seeking the help I need not to do it again.

Joy comes not through effort but through awareness.

Joy is simple. Joy is medicine for healing wounds. The potential to tap it is always there, though I am not always able to open myself to that belief. I often convince myself that it will take hours, days, years to come out of my darkness, and this becomes a self-fulfilling prophecy that takes me back to the feelings I had when I was being abused. Actually, joy can be just around a corner.

As I grow stronger and more balanced, I become aware that I can look for joy. When I hear a voice telling me life is joyless, I can dispute it by beginning a gratitude list. I can look around at the simple things in my life that bring joy, such as my pets, the birds at the bird feeder, a painting on the wall. If I allow it, I will feel the place in my heart where these simple things find meaning, even if the place of bleakness still remains right beside it.

When I separate from my abusive family, I
may feel bereft before I feel better, even though
I am doing what is right for me.

Separating by its nature causes a shift inside
us. It comes with feelings of being fragmented,
for we are dismantling an old foundation. We
may be taking a positive step for ourselves by initiating a separation, but we will not feel immediate relief or fulfillment. Instead, we may feel the
pain of withdrawal as strong as we would feel it if
we were in our first few days without a drug we
had become addicted to. This reaction will go
away with time. We do not need to doubt our decision each time we feel it, but simply let our ambivalence play out in us until it wanes.

I can make a decision for my own good and
follow through on it. Living with a degree of ambivalence is a measure of my maturity, not a confirmation that I have made a mistake. By sitting
still through my uncomfortable feelings, I deepen
my relationship to myself.

I encourage myself to grow up, despite messages I still hear to remain passive and dependent.

Much of my independent and assertive side was compromised by the abuse I received. I felt flawed because I was unable to stop the perpetrator. It seemed as if my inability to cry out and tell someone was the reason why it happened or continued. This picture of me, stuck and unable to express myself, dominated my sense of who I was and left me small and unable to fight for myself.

Today I allow myself to speak out about the incest, at least to myself and to others who understand. I find and express my rage at the perpetrators. I determine whether I want or need to confront them, and how to do it in my best interest. I recognize my rage holds much of the energy I need to assert myself as a growing adult. I permit myself to own it. It is time for me to move with the flow of my life, to leave behind the dependency my family fostered in me. Even if I encounter some static in myself, it is time to encourage myself to become who I want to be.

I choose what sort of relationship I want to have with my family of origin today.

I was deeply wounded as a child growing up in an abusive family situation. I also have profound attachments to the members of my family.

Chances are that members of my family have not changed their attitudes even though I have been working to change mine. They may still try to treat me abusively by ignoring me or humiliating me. But today I do not need to take this treatment from anyone. I have choices. The choices may feel extreme—either cut them off completely or put up with them—but if I take a closer look I see there are options in between. For instance, I might try a policy of visiting them only when accompanied by a friend who understands what I have been through. I might put a time limit on my visits. Or I might tell them I cannot be in contact at all while I am focused on my healing.

Some of us choose to completely sever with our family as the best medicine for our healing. Some of us choose to return to them but from a new position of strength and confidence in ourselves. Some of us eventually forgive and feel compassion for how our parents too were probably abused before us and, unable to find avenues for healing, perpetuated this injury.

In solitude, my soul gets restored.

To truly know myself, I must be able to sit still quietly alone, let interior clutter fall away, and hear the voice of my spirit. Many of us have difficulty achieving this, incest survivors or not. But if I had my solitude interrupted by abusive intrusions as a child, or if I had to isolate myself to escape from being victimized, it may be even harder for me.

In my healing I learn to distinguish between isolation and solitude. In isolation I act to barricade myself from other people. I surround myself with the internal voices that are generally bad company for me to keep. In solitude I make a choice to be alone without the din of these voices. I open myself to my spirit as it is in the present moment. I let distractions pass through without giving them credence. I respect the integrity of my soul.

Today I will allow a new healthy sexuality to exist and grow in me along with my freedom to express it.

My sexuality was distorted and repressed by my incest experience. I felt that sexual feelings were always connected with being exploited or hurt or being a powerless victim. I experienced my own sexual responses as fraught with the potential to betray my true self, since the stimulation I felt during the incest left me confused.

In my healing I will reclaim my natural responses. I need to choose a partner who will allow me the emotional space to stay with my feelings a day at a time. I need to give myself permission to be only as sexual as I feel like being at any given time. To push beyond or in a different direction from the impulses of my body will lead me to feel revictimized.

I visualize myself fully deserving of a rich and full sexuality, and I seek out the environment that can offer me a place to experience my God-given sexuality. Celibacy is an option that I may choose for a short or a long time. It is up to me to decide what is right for me. I will follow my instincts and listen to those who have gone before me.

I can choose to explore and express myself through masks and costumes without abandoning my true self.

In my childhood I needed to put on a mask or a costume to disguise myself. I needed to create a persona I could feel safe in—the athlete, the dramatist, the high achiever. While I protected myself by keeping my core wrapped in a cocoon and held dormant for later attention, I hid myself well from others while also being hidden from myself.

In my healing I gradually risk moving out of any and all personas and simply present me as me. This takes time and discovery, for I have been deeply shrouded and will need repeated attention to know me simply as me. I give myself opportunities for exploration. I can try out different haircuts, different clothing, until I find exactly what suits me.

Halloween can be a time to design an ingenious costume that allows me to experiment with a chosen persona. I can use this opportunity to move closer to my real self, even while donning a mask that might appear illusory.

November

Even when I feel harried and distressed, I can stay on course by doing the next right thing. I do not need to capsize.

As I recover the ability to feel my feelings, they often seem overwhelming. My impulse might be to have the temper tantrums I stuffed as a child or to collapse utterly into my sorrow. Often I hear a voice say, "Give up. You can't handle this." And since I had little guidance as a child in how to keep rolling along with my feelings, it is not surprising that I have an impulse to derail and shut down.

In my healing I realize that feelings do not need to stop or slow my progress. In fact, they can fuel me when I integrate them into my daily activities. Even in distress I can take care of business. I can keep all aspects of my life operating. To intercept the signal for defeat in being overwhelmed, I look for guidance for the next right thing to do. I listen for the suggestion that will lead me to balance.

*I will first learn to trust my own instincts and
then risk trusting others who have proved
themselves reliable.*

I trusted people in my childhood who betrayed and invaded me. I was wounded by the
betrayal and then further wounded because there
was no acknowledgment of it. Instead it was
denied and made secret. If my response to this
betrayal was rage, this too had to be hidden.
From then on, there was always a false bottom in
my ability to trust. Sometimes I made myself vulnerable by being overly trusting of others; other
times I was lonely as the result of trusting no one.

Today I begin anew to develop a willingness to
trust in a way that first and foremost takes *me*
into account. I trust my feelings will protect me,
but I must explore them as they come and not
jump to conclusions. In an intimate situation it
will feel risky to trust another. Yet I *can* do so. I
can reassure my inner child that I am keeping my
eyes open and will continue to express myself. I
can detach and hold to my own course when
someone close seems to want to control me. I can
move in and out of complete trust of another and
count on my instincts to guide me wisely.

My fear of being loved does not prove me unlovable. It is simply a measure of my fragility.

We all deserve to be loved now. We also deserved to receive love in our childhood. But many of us encountered cruel substitutes, such as seduction and betrayal, triangulation between our parents, neglect and humiliation for allowing our needs to show. We did not have a chance to develop a sense of love as a flowing energy. Instead, we became sensitized to the conditions we had to play to for almost any attention, which we mistook for love.

To be loved now I need to let go of old definitions, which were never true anyway. There is no finite quantity to love; it regenerates by flowing. As I give it, I receive it. In fear my energy stops, as if against a dam. It is then I have the opportunity to realize I am new and tender and in unfamiliar territory. My discomfort does not mean anything is wrong. By attending to my fragility, I find my resilience.

*Under no circumstances do I need to tolerate
anyone's abuse of me, whether they intend it or
not.*

Having lived through abuse as a child, I grew
up with the impression that two people cannot
function together in a nonabusive way. Abuse
seemed the inevitable consequence of conflict. I
have little idea of how people solve their differ-
ences respectfully. I have gone round and round
the same track with relationships, eventually feeling victimized and not seeing a clear vision of
how to function without abuse.

Today new options exist for me. I make the
choice to exit from abuse whenever it occurs in
my presence. I know it is right for me to create
safe conditions in which to resolve conflict. Saying no to someone does not mean I have to bear
the brunt of the rejected person's temper tantrum. I am not responsible if another loses control. I am responsible for protecting myself. I can
let it be known that I am concerned about the
other person's feelings without becoming a
punching bag for him or her. I can leave but des-
ignate a time I will return—after a cooling-off
period—to continue to resolve the conflict.

My old ways die like leaves in the fall, leaving me naked. Then I open to healing.

My wounds are deep. Even though I managed to put them out of my awareness for many years, they remained raw because they were untended. Until I tended to them, I found a narrow swatch of land on which I could travel, ignoring them but not without great cost to my spaciousness and freedom.

As I consciously recover from sexual abuse, I encounter deep pain and tenderness in my wounds. I realize the black hole inside me is nothing more than my injury. It can no longer be ignored or evaded. I enter into it with the help of my higher power and my sister survivors. I touch it. I feel deep sadness for how much of my childhood was lived in darkness. I share with others what it was like. Though I may see no light as I take these first steps, in spite of my despair, gradually I will see the dawn coming. I will feel new and vulnerable, as if something was shifted. I will look in my heart and see that where it has been touched, it is healing.

*My frustration tolerance grows as I allow
myself to know that my periods of darkness
always pass.*

When things do not go my way, I am easily be-
wildered. I become frustrated. I may see myself
as trapped. I flash back to painful times of being
victimized and cannot sit quietly until the outlines and meaning of what is happening emerge
more clearly. I panic instead, fearing the feelings
of the abuse—of having someone else control or
dominate me.

It helps to know that these difficult moments
will pass. It helps to say the Serenity Prayer. Have
I done all I can do? If I have, then I am free to let
go of effort. I do not need to fear that I will be
stuck in a place of great frustration. I need only
pray for guidance to see what door is being
opened. Then I realize I never needed to cling to
my will so tenaciously in the first place. It is my
higher power's will for me I am seeking to understand.

*When I acknowledge my fear of success, it loses
its power to hold me up and rob me.*

The abusive experiences of my childhood
knocked me down, and I felt like a failure because of being mistreated. My strong desire to become a success in some aspect of life became my
way to prove that I am not a failure and counter-
act these feelings. I see now this drive was taking
me away from, not toward, wholeness. For I was
going to be a success to escape the fact I had been
injured.

When we try to function at cross-purposes
with ourselves, we are liable to trip ourselves up.
If this results in failure, we are brought back to
look closer at where we went wrong. Have we neglected our spiritual values out of greed for material success or public recognition? Have we
abandoned the needs of our inner child out of a
false conception of how to exit from our painful
past?

I will follow the guidance of my higher power
and look for the next right thing, trusting that the
plan for my success will gradually be shown to
me. I will know a new freedom from fear. This in
itself I may come to experience as true success.

I no longer allow the voice of my perpetrator to keep me from taking action.

I have many talents and have often been able to develop them up to a point, but have then felt stymied when it came to taking further action. For instance, I might have been able to work with my skills and imagination to make fine paintings, yet been unable to mobilize myself to find any way to have them seen and recognized by others. I might be the best worker at my job and yet feel unqualified to compete for the supervisor's position when it becomes vacant.

In recovery I begin to comprehend what always puzzled me before—how others less competent were able to look after themselves much better than I was. It never made sense to me. Now I realize I was held back by the internalized messages of my perpetrator: "You're not worth it. You're tainted. Your value is questionable at best. The more you go for it, the more I'll get you."

I no longer let this voice speak uninterrupted. I know it does not contribute to my well-being. I talk back and learn to go ahead with my actions.

I will speak my truth and stand firmly for my-self despite threats or threatening feelings.

In my childhood there were grave conse-quences when I tried to speak my truth. I was threatened overtly and covertly by family mem-bers. My survival depended on my silence. I honor and respect the defenses I used as a child, but today I need to recognize that my situation has changed.

I often erect barriers inside myself and feel that I am not free to speak over them. Yet to heal I must do so. I must speak the truth of my feelings over and over again. In doing so I become alive. I am free to choose wisely when and where to speak out. Sometimes I may only need to speak to myself and my higher power to recognize what is troubling me. Sometimes I will need to talk with another person; still other times I may need to confront someone who has hurt me. It will re-quire time and experience to consistently make the appropriate choices. I will allow myself to make mistakes and learn from them without chastising myself as a failure. Instead, I will ground myself in the awareness that I am in a process and will allow myself to feel the clarity of my truth.

Fearing the unknown within myself has kept me crouching in a corner. I look to see who I am and discover much that is worthy.

Many of us who were abused as children were taught a belief system in which we were shameful. "Shame on you! . . ." "You should be ashamed of yourself!" were frequent refrains for the slightest infraction. Add to this the fact that our abusers heaped shame on us for the incest itself and it is easy to see why we might have lived our life as if we were wreckage buried under a mountain of shame for many years.

As I recover I take stock of who I really am. When I am afraid to look, I realize I can use the tools I have learned to walk ahead even with fear. I can pray for awareness of my higher power's presence. I can distinguish past history from the present and recognize I am dealing with shame that has masked a truer picture of myself. I can give back what belongs to others. When I do that, it prepares me for the freedom to truly know myself. I will be amazed at the pleasure to be had in doing this. I will delight in my discoveries.

I give up my wish to control everything and accept the things I cannot change.

I cannot change the fact that I am a survivor of childhood sexual abuse. I cannot rewrite my past and leave that out. Often I've tried to handle it this way because I knew no other way. At least appearing to believe I had a trustworthy parent seemed the only way to go on when I was a child. But today I want to stand my ground by standing on the truth.

Today I work to recognize and accept life as it is and to realize resisting reality only consumes energy I can better use to take care of myself. For instance, when I am ill, the sooner I surrender to my powerlessness over the illness and attend to myself, the sooner I will be restored to the best possible health.

When I bulldoze my way through a day without regard to what is truly mine to change, I can create the illusion that I am going somewhere, but I will surely not have the satisfaction of serenity. Yet with acceptance, even in the midst of duress, I can know peace.

*My body is free to enjoy sexual feelings; I learn
to differentiate these feelings from love.*

The life force is energy—yours, mine, the
earth's and all her creatures. We are bound together with the force of life. When we are sexually attracted to someone, energy reverberates in
us and flows to our genitals.

Sexual feelings may have been aroused in us as
children when we were being abused. This does
not mean we were attracted to the perpetrator or
the situation, which was one of being held hostage. Our arousal was a natural reaction to having
erectile tissues stimulated and we had no control
over it. It does not make us guilty.

In my healing I learn to let sexual feelings flow
through me and enjoy them without getting
scrambled signals. I recognize that the energy of
love and the energy of lust can sometimes feel
similar, but I am capable of making necessary
distinctions to separate them. Every time I feel attracted, I do not need to imagine that this means
I have found the next person I should relate to.

I allow my faith to sow the seeds that will let me recognize failed and frustrating behaviors and bring me to change.

I am reluctant to admit my failed and frustrating behaviors, but when I look at how long I have done something the same way, despite the fact that it does not work, I see that this is not sensible behavior. If I could have changed before now on my own, I believe I would have done so. What a relief then to now let in the possibility that a power greater than myself exists and might restore me to sanity.

As an incest survivor, I learned to absorb enormous abuse. I learned to soak up the anger of others. I learned to go deep inside myself for protection, cutting off from my feelings so that others could not hurt me so badly. While this protected me, it also damaged me by depriving me of the ability to know and show my feelings. I had to try to keep everything under control.

As I recover and release the illusion of control, I need the help of my higher power to truly let go and to see that new doors are opening.

*I have chosen a path that requires awakening to
deeper and deeper levels of honesty in myself.*

In an abusive family system, survival often requires lying. Being honest about our feelings may
have made us subject to punishment. Growing
up in such a system, we learned to value saying
the thing that would placate someone over our
own need to tell the truth.

Even in recovery I feel vulnerable about being
truthful. I gradually become more aware that hiding my feelings from others has also kept them
hidden from me. As my self-esteem grows, I comprehend that I no longer have any reason to live
in the darkness of lies. I can tell the truth about
myself because there is nothing wrong with me as
I am, even though I may have times of distress,
anger, neediness.

I give myself the gift of compassion for the
times I was unable to be honest. I allow myself
now to continue to shed one layer after another
as my search goes deeper and deeper. I may fear
the unknown inside myself, but the longer I go
on looking, the more I see I have nothing to fear.

I learn to take care of myself at both ends of the spectrum, when I am in angst and when I am thriving.

When someone sought to take care of me as a child, it was only in sporadic bursts. Thus I learned early on to rely on the idea that being taken care of was a stroke of good luck, not reliable. This has made it difficult for me to focus on learning to be consistent in self-care. Am I able to reach out only when I am in the most severe pain? If I do the right thing to take care of myself, do I then subject myself to inner torment, as if I must become a substitute for the tormentor who abused me as a child?

I yearn for the freedom to be myself and to give myself a life free of torment. I attain this a day at a time by practicing the gift of self-care. As soon as I notice I am limiting myself—"You just gave yourself a treat yesterday, today you should deprive yourself to make up for it" or "It's not bad enough yet to call for help"—I simply observe the thought and let it drift away from me. Then I ask what care is needed and allow myself to have it.

To make order without and within, I will seek peace of mind, and trust I need only do first things first.

When I feel confused and am behind in all that appears to need to be done, I will stop a moment and reflect on my priorities. Have I been neglecting some aspect of myself? Am I in touch with the fear of the child within me? Do I trust my higher power? Am I running away from my feelings? For when time feels speeded up it is usually due to my being out of sync with myself.

Because of my incest experience, I went into hiding. I hid to survive. I still often fall into thinking I am safer if I hide and am not truly present, but my recovery tells me I am safest when I come out and am fully present and aware.

When I feel disorderly, I will sit still and allow my higher power to guide me to the next right thing to be handled. What emerges may surprise me. It might be cleaning up my house. Or it might be working on a more internal housekeeping.

I give as an expression of love for my being.

Giving is a simple, pure way of expressing my loving feelings if I do not mix it up with other motivations.

Growing up in a family in which there was overt and covert sexual abuse, giving may have been as misused as every expression of connection was. We may have felt "bought" by a parent's giving. We may have felt seduced or manipulated because something special was being given to us while we were being sexually objectified and abused. We may have had a parent who withdrew and withheld affection or other gifts, leaving us feeling neglected. Or one who set us up to compete with siblings for the gift of their scarce attention.

In my recovery I seek to emerge from these ways—which have cloaked pure giving with excess baggage—and practice giving as a message from my heart. It is in this way that I will come to witness and experience the fullness I receive from my own generosity.

*I enjoy feeling protected by my higher power
and by the people who love me.*

Many of us felt betrayed as children, not only
by our perpetrators but by those who we perceived should have protected us. One parent may
have cowered in the face of the other's abuse,
looking away from it, denying it was happening,
or buying into the notion that we had done
something to deserve it. This parent seemed unconscious, oblivious to the fact that abuse was
going on. Instead he or she may have busily created the myth of the idealized family or zoned
out on alcohol. Regardless of that parent's mode,
we were left unprotected and this neglect compounded the harm of our abuse.

Consequently, it may still be difficult to let myself be and feel protected. I have created a network of supportive friends and healing people
around me. I have turned myself and my will
over to the care of my higher power. I am no
longer alone and unprotected. I need only open
myself to feel the cushion of protection that exists
in my world today. I make a conscious effort to
let it in and allow it to contribute to my healing.

*Even if the abuse I suffered from a sibling was
directed by a parent or other authority figure, I
can still come out of the fog and hold my sibling
accountable for his or her actions.*

Many of us suffered sexual abuse from one or
more of our older siblings. In some cases, because we detect that they were either imitating a
parent or taking direction from one, it is hard to
hold them accountable. But if we check in with
our inner child and ask her to tell us just how she
was wounded, we may find that some of our
deepest pain comes from how we were treated by
a sibling. The fact that we may have relied on a
sibling for a sense of connection and protection
within the family also makes it hard to let ourselves realize the damages.

I need to let myself come out of the fog and
remember the whole of my experience with my
sibling. I was hurt when my sibling professed to
help me out, then tantalized me by making me
jump through hoops for them. Even while I can
see that they protected themselves from the pain
of being victimized by adopting or supporting
the role of the abuser, I am outraged at how I was
wounded by their behavior. I need to admit and
express this before I can heal.

I will take the time to clear up hazy or confused communication rather than leaving myself or others in doubt.

Speech is one of the tools that has been given to me so that I may reach out from my separateness and connect with other people. I use words from my own experience, knowing my own meaning. I often speak to another person from within my experience without being aware that my mind cannot be so fully known by another as it is by myself. Sometimes then my communication is partial, indirect, or does not truly express what I would like it to.

In my incest experience I was silenced; communicating my feelings was absolutely not welcomed. Thus, I fear no one wants to know how I truly feel. This leads me, even today, to try to communicate indirectly. Instead of saying right out what I want or need, I go fishing to test the responsiveness of other people. But this only confuses and sets off feelings of inadequacy in other people for not being able to understand my faulty communication.

When I speak directly and openly of my needs and feelings, I may be surprised to find them quite easily understood.

*I grow responsive to my individual needs. Any
guilt that arises as a result of my caring for
them belongs in the dump.*

As victims of incest we were forced to forgo
our individuality to satisfy someone else's needs.
Our perpetrators conveniently used a position of
authority in the family to impose their interests
and desires on us when we did not share those
interests and desires. We were being sacrificed.
Any move we made to establish an individual
identity was threatening to this system and
treated as punishable. We learned to keep our
mouths shut and hide our individuality.

As I heal I identify my own needs and respond
to the desire to have them met. Because of the ab-
sence of reinforcement for them in my past, I will
often feel guilty when I step forward on my own
behalf. I understand this guilt comes from the
voices that are activated when I step out of the
old ways of my family. I will as gently as possible
load this guilt on a wheelbarrow and drop it off at
the dump. Responding to my needs and growing
stronger as an individual is a fine thing to behold.
I applaud it.

I seek a therapist who I sense can support me.

My relationship with a therapist is a primary component of my healing. I need to take the time and give myself permission to search until I have found the right one. I do not need to stick with anyone who I do not intuitively feel can hear and help me. I am entitled to seek information about the therapist to determine her or his qualifications in general, and more specifically regarding the areas I want to work with, such as sexual abuse.

Many of us who've been abused have been conditioned to believe that we are lazy or evasive and will only work when someone holds a whip over us. It may seem alien to us to choose a therapist who supports us consistently, even though we sometimes feel we are unworthy of support. We may even feel this proves our therapist is a fool. We must guard against recreating the abuse of the past with a therapist. We need and deserve to be supported. We can choose this even if it feels uncomfortable. With time it will feel right.

Today I want the maturity and stability that come from living in the present.

In my past I needed to find ways to avoid reality or alter my sense of it. It was too painful to tolerate reality. And one of my parents fed me a make-pretend version of our family life as exemplary. I grew up and spent years fogged out of reality by abusing myself with alcohol and other drugs.

What I notice today is that while my perceptions change with my moods and feelings, reality stays constant. It can become a reassuring anchor if I let it. For instance, one aspect of reality is that I am an adult now, and I need not fear that I will have to encounter my childhood traumas again. I need to return to them in memory, and may even need to experience the feelings about them at a more intense level than I did when I was a child. But I am not there. I am safe in the now as long as I take care to protect myself and stay in reality.

*To accept the losses of my childhood and begin
to put my abuse in the past, I will need to
grieve those losses.*

As I realize the neglect I encountered in my
childhood—the lack of love, of normal cuddling,
of safe and trusting feelings—I am overwhelmed
by my losses. I do not want to feel the pain of recognizing that I was so bereft, yet I see the sadness
in pictures of the young me and I want to offer
the truth to that child.

Grief is not a single emotion but a mix of feelings. It may contain rage, loneliness, confusion,
profound sadness. I may fear some part of me is
dying and I will not be able to survive without it.
I may feel that to admit the full extent of my
losses will leave me too thin-skinned for life.
Here I must call upon the faith I have developed,
which has shown me again and again how clearing out the old makes room for the new.

In grief I experience vacancy—a space inside
that was formerly cluttered becomes empty. It
may not come dramatically or all at once, but
gradually what trickles in to fill me is my hard-
won freedom.

I am thankful today and every day for the opportunity I've been given to open myself to a bountiful life.

I do not need to deny the deprivations and injuries of the past to recognize that right now my life is full of opportunities to realize abundance. Being aware of my past in a truthful way helps me let go of the feeling that it is surrounding me still and dictating my life's direction. It gives me a strong foundation for owning the experiences and feelings that went into forming who I am and how I react today. It lets me bring myself up to the present.

When I look around in the present, I realize my cup is full. There is love in my heart for myself and for others. I have parted with the isolation of having to keep secrets about my incest and shared with others who have had similar experiences. I've come to believe that a power greater than myself is ever present and available whenever I turn to her. This belief, in itself a great bounty, allows me to trust I never need to return to being boarded up like an old haunted house. I give thanks today for my well-being.

I am free to choose the sexual identity that fits me.

Lesbian, heterosexual, bisexual, celibate; butch, femme, or adrogyne—the right sexual identity is the one that suits me, not the one I might choose to please others. I let myself intuitively come into this knowledge.

When we first crack the secrets surrounding our sexual abuse, many of us question our sexual identity. If our mother was our abuser, would that make us lesbian? Or would it make us feel safer with men and therefore orient us heterosexually? As we go further in our recovery, we look around in our groups and see that nothing seems to correlate. There are survivors of all orientations.

If I have questions about my sexual identity, I give myself the freedom to explore them. Because of homophobic attitudes in the society at large, I may associate shame with homosexuality. If I separate this shame from the shame of the abuse, I will be better able to clarify my direction.

Today I have a relationship with my body in which I notice its pain, its pleasure, and other cues it gives me about how I feel.

For years I divorced myself from my body as if it were a nuisance. I did not want to listen when it tried to tell me something. Because of my incest I learned early in life how to split off from it and let its pain exist as if it were separate from me. This was a tool of survival.

If I had a pain in the neck, I cursed it, medicated it, and tried to get away from it. If I had a headache, I let my life contract around it until I became less active and felt sorry for myself. Never did I attend to my body by turning my heart and mind to it, asking what it needed to tell me or what it wanted me to give it.

As I heal I recognize my body is a valuable treasury of memories. Physical pain can signal real danger. It can also reflect psychic pain, and when this is the case and I turn to recognize it, my body breathes a deep sigh of relief and stops hurting. I am grateful today for the integrity of my body, and I am learning to trust its ability to express things I am not yet consciously able to handle.

*I permit myself to show up just as I am and will
not let the voices of perfectionism put me down
as a failure.*

Perfectionism can be self-abusive. If I delude
myself into believing I can correct the mistake
that must have led to my abuse, I am still holding
on to the message that I caused the abuse and am
unworthy.

I may drive myself unduly to perform and
achieve to prove my worthiness. If I seek positive
reinforcement for my worthiness only in this way,
it may be entrapping, because I am not then free
to stop and exercise other aspects of myself without risking the loss of this approval.

In my recovery I am becoming aware of who I
am in all respects. I seek to integrate all parts of
myself into a full person whose worthiness grows
from within. I no longer wish to occupy a particular persona, even if it would appear to make me
shine in some situation. I choose to attend life
with my whole self, sometimes faltering, sometimes confident. When I put this principle into
practice, the rewards will be apparent in my
heart.

I will not be tripped up because of my sexual attraction to someone, or the knowledge of someone's attraction to me.

This problem may be common even to some who are not sexual abuse survivors, but we who were abused in childhood are especially prone to being confused by feelings of sexual attraction. If someone seems to care for us and beams loving attention on us, our body may respond with sexual attraction even though this person is not someone we want to have a sexual relationship with. If someone says, "I have a crush on you," we may feel the need to respond with, "I think I'm in love with you," even when we aren't. We may feel as if wires are crossing in our brains.

I have sometimes ended up in long-term relationships after a beginning like this, which did not allow for a calm assessment and exploration of compatibility. The very feeling of being tripped up I mistook for the sensation of falling in love. Real love does not need to be snared quickly but will allow me all the time I need. I recognize that my incest has distorted my perceptions and created a web of confusion about pleasure, love, and sexual feelings. I take the time I need to sort through this confusion.

When I feel overwhelmed, I will slow down and return to a receptive relationship with my higher power.

When changes occur in my outer life, time feels speeded up. I begin to doubt how it will be possible for everything to fall in place as I need it to. I grasp at my will to try to achieve some security. But I find myself without serenity.

In my incest experience, I was powerless and hated feeling that way. I did not choose to surrender; I was forced to surrender. This now contributes to my reluctance to trust that I can safely turn my will over to the care of my higher power.

But I can begin by trying to allow my life to be simpler. I can open myself to following a Good Orderly Direction, and this in itself may come to feel like a representation of GOD. I will be able to follow this path peacefully as soon as I have aligned myself with God. Then I will find myself guided to the next right thing to take care of.

December

*I visualize the relationship of profound mutual
love and support I would like to have.*

I am fully entitled to a mutually loving, caring
relationship, but I may not be able to have it exactly when I want it. While this feels frustrating,
I can consider the idea that my higher power
knows the right time for me when I am incapable
of knowing it myself.

I am free to visualize what I want at any time.
Doing so may help me recognize areas that I can
choose to work on. For instance, in my visualization do I know the qualities I would like to see in
the other person? Do I run into blank spots when
I imagine being loved and cared for? Do I yearn
for a true peer and yet feel uneasy at the notion of
equality because I have satisfied my desire for
control out of being the protector in past relationships? Do I realize my sexual abuse has
trapped me into acting out of a need to either
have power over others or be someone's victim?

My visualization will allow me to see where I
need to continue healing. I will grow stronger
with time and more able to know when I am
truly ready for a love relationship.

When I am fearful of using my talents to the fullest, I will remember that they have been given to me as gifts from God.

Because my incest forced me into hiding, because with attention I also encountered devastating abuse, my inner child long ago decided it would be best to retreat and go unnoticed. This left me unable to go forth with my talents when to do so might mean receiving public attention.

Today I realize I am not living in a situation in which I am subject to abuse, unless I allow it to happen to me. I have God-given talents to develop. When I foster and nourish them, I feel my spirit rising. I no longer need to hold back out of fear of becoming visible. I need to express myself in the ways that were given to me. When I do so, I may still feel great discomfort because my inner child will be anxious that I am making myself vulnerable. Rather than ignore her, I share the anxiety with my therapist and other survivors, pay attention to my feelings, and allow myself to gain confidence that I am learning to take care of myself and moving to use my talents.

I seek and find ways to envision my higher power's presence so that I can readily tap this source.

Learning to trust in a power greater than ourselves is a great challenge for many of us. When we were children, our parents were powers greater than us and in many cases misused this advantage. Even if we received religious instruction about a god, we may have already felt quite sure our only chance of survival was to not trust anyone or anything but ourselves.

In recovery I see how others find comfort and guidance in a higher power. I begin to desire and feel deserving of having such a presence in my life too. I am free to make my own personal connections with this presence. I do not need to envision it in any conventional form. Yet I yearn to develop some way to picture my higher power so that my concept of it is not entirely abstract.

I may describe my higher power as a force I share with my sister survivors. I may imagine a Goddess who I call to my room to pray to. I may go outdoors and envision the colors and forms of nature as the embodiment of this power. I locate the images that are meaningful to me today.

I will replace old messages of deprivation with recognition of the abundance in my life.

Because of the abuse I received, I felt downtrodden, injured, and victimized. Yet because the abuse had to be kept secret, how could I show how I felt on the outside? What better way to show the world how my life lacked enrichment than to live in a deprived way, being an underearner, an underachiever, or never allowing myself a vacation without guilt?

As I begin to heal I see that my self-depriving ways only reinforce the impression that I am undeserving. I vow to ask myself regularly what I want and need. I learn to allot money and time to myself in ways that can fulfill my desires. As I do this I recognize the potential for thinking in a radically different way—with the concept of abundance. I release myself from the old idea that there will never be enough for me and begin to notice the areas of my life that are abundant. Even if I am not financially solvent, I have good food, adequate clothing, and a warm home. I have a fine view of the sunset, loving friends, and a clear mind. These are all elements of abundance if I allow them to qualify.

*I am willing to return to experiences that were
so painful I dissociated myself from them.*

I did not choose to dissociate one part of myself from another. This occurred as a defense
when I encountered traumas too great for me to
handle as a helpless child, when my personality
was not yet sufficiently formed to protest, even in
thought.

Those of us who split off parts of ourselves this
way cannot feel whole without returning to integrate them. Our split fragments remain anchored
in the past and want to draw us back there. To
connect with them we must accept the experiences we have so carefully sought to conceal. We
must expose them and recognize them.

We are okay now to do this, strong and supported enough to release our outrage. Our hatred
can be let out and will cease then to poison us
and we will have peace of mind.

When I begin to feel dominated by a crisis, I will pay attention to caring for all the spheres of my life until I am restored to balance.

In a crisis all my energy rapidly moves off to cling ferociously to the one thing I perceive as the problem, as if focusing my attention so exclusively will guarantee the solution. But like a washing machine thrown out of kilter, I go round and round in my own distorted circuits until I find a way to let go and redistribute my energy.

During the abuse, I felt I achieved some control by clutching madly to the crisis, but I got stuck here, waiting for someone else to recognized the crisis, while no one did. Today I can see this as a form of insanity and give myself the freedom to experiment with new ways.

I can look on my self and my needs as portions of a pie—with spiritual, physical, emotional, and intellectual pieces. I can attend to each piece without neglecting the others. Whatever crisis throws me out of kilter, I will see more clearly if I see it from a perspective of harmony and balance within me.

I ask for the strength to release my voice and allow the expression of all that is in me.

Expressing my feelings was threatening to others in my family's abusive system. Consequently, I learned to suppress them or turn them in against myself. One of my jobs as an incest survivor is to learn how to reverse this inward turning and find effective expression.

My initial actions will be fraught with trepidation, for this is a case of a childhood survival tactic turning into an adult liability. I may feel foolish or vulnerable, but I can ask for the support I need to move the expression of my feelings outward, such as talking before and after my actions to others who understand me. In receiving their support, I nurture the development in myself that was not nurtured in my childhood. With each act I feel my power growing and I become more comfortable with it. I come to know and appreciate the release inside me that comes with a more appropriate outer-directed expression of my feelings.

I am alive with the vitality of the present; my past no longer flattens me.

The horrifying and humiliating abuse experiences I encountered as a child will never happen to me again. I survived them, learning effective defenses that helped me. But these defenses flattened me too, for remaining fully open to my feelings would have been devastating.

If I have reached the point in my healing where the defenses feel like excess baggage trailing along behind me, I am ready to let them go. When fear comes, I remind myself I am safe now. I have developed into an adult who can adequately protect herself. I do not need to shut down my feelings.

As I let down the shields I have hidden my feelings behind, I feel vital. I realize how excited I can be about the simple lovely gifts of life. I feel the energy that has been held back within me bubbling to the surface. I embrace it.

I will turn to my higher power when I am over-whelmed by fear of my powerlessness.

I was powerless over my abuse. I may have felt that my higher power abandoned me and allowed me to be wounded in that way. I needed to abandon my body to preserve its dignity. Nonetheless, my spirit remained intact even when I was unable to experience it as so.

It is said that fear and faith cannot live in the same house. When I feel my powerlessness, I will turn with trust to my higher power and pray for the guidance to believe I am in her care. I will open my heart to receive the love that is there for me, even if I do not feel I can love myself. A million excuses clamor to tell me why this is not a good time to surrender, that I had best manipulate my life into a better position first. But I am learning from my new experiences that a good time to surrender is now. I can get off at any floor; I do not have to wait until I am desperate. I see that my success rate for working my way out of fear without help has not been very impressive. Asking for help cannot possibly harm me, so why would I not do it?

I create a home that is a safe and nurturing place for me, where I am free to gather myself.

In my family of origin I did not feel safe in my home. If I managed to create small spaces where I felt safe, they did not allow much room for expansion. For instance, I played in a closet or hung out for hours with my dollhouse where I fantasized the children were safe and secure.

Today I realize I have a right to make a home for myself that is both safe and pleasing. I decorate it in a way that represents me. If I share it with others, I honor my need to have some separate space that I can call my own. With time I feel rooted in my home. My energy and some of my history is centered there.

It is not my wish to stay home so much that I become isolated, but to use the comforting influence of my home to restore and gather myself after each step I take in my expanding ability to participate in the world. I am a world citizen. My home is not an island but a place that reinforces me.

Fire is energy; it can destroy or inspire.

We watch a fire, matter combusting. It snaps and crackles. Its roar scorches the listener's ear. We are excited by it even while we are frightened and wish it would stop.

The fire within me is the vortex of my energy. It flashes my rage momentarily before me. My passion is at its center. I reach for it, desirous. I want what is mine, why shouldn't I? But the flames push me away and make me cower. My outrage pours out bit by bit, finding expression. I watch how others do this too—beating on pillows, screaming and howling out the offense of the abused child still residing within, standing fast in the refusal to tolerate further abuse.

When shame no longer finds a home in my body, my fire will ignite inspiration, as happens when I dream through a feverish sleep.

The air teaches me about stillness and motion and how each has its place in nature.

Air is always in our presence. We often focus ourselves through breathing, by noticing how the air passes into and out of our lungs, by how the deeper we breathe, the more we move out of our survival stance and into an expansive state of being.

I can relate to air both as the element that gives me life and as a source for change. The wind blows in and swirls up a storm, then passes to stillness. In me also there are storms of emotions that tend to feel never-ending when they are present. A deep sigh may remind me that they, too, shall pass.

The past deeply imprints us and certainly matters, yet it is important for me to realize that life has a continuous flow and I am part of that. I ritually give to the wind the pain I have worked through, the pain I am ready to part with.

Today I show up for my life and attempt to live in the present moment as best I can.

One way I survived my incest experience was to exit from the present reality. Grateful as I am for this tactic and how it spared me in some way, it no longer serves me. It takes me away to the past or future, away from the richness of the moment that is here right now. If I stay only in the present moment, chances are there is nothing all that threatening coming at me. If I hover in the past or try to predict the future, my fears are bound to be aroused and begin old voices talking.

If I stay with what my present moment offers, there is always much to be grateful for—the natural beauty around me, the smile of another, a tasty meal, the warmth of the sun, the affection of a pet. Almost any small detail can show me how I am provided for if only I care to see it. I can appreciate even the uncomfortable feelings I may be having in the present moment. For we all have pain. I am a human among humans and to know and be present with my pain allows me to know others with theirs.

Instead of clamoring for attention, I can turn to myself, comprehend what I need at this moment, and allow myself to have it.

When my needs go unmet, I am likely to make excess noise in an attempt to be heard. Slamming a door, vying competitively for attention, becoming a mascot for the amusement of others, having a temper tantrum—these can all be cries for attention. But they do not get me what I need—genuine care for my wounds.

In my family of origin the tactics for getting attention were competitive. Attention came in a limited and short supply. It was dispersed only if vied for. One needed to develop a strategy for getting ahead of others or going without.

Today I know that I have all I need to take care of myself. The reason it remains a struggle is because a battle ensues inside me when I seek to remove myself from the old family patterns. This battle takes away my peace of mind. But I can float a ship for peace even when there is worrisome energy all around me. I can close a door quietly and have a look inside myself to see what needs caring for.

I recognize the powerlessness of worry to protect me, and I allow myself to relax.

As small children we were once innocent, playful, and exploratory. We thought the world revolved around us. We poked around, touching and testing and being gleeful with our sensations. When we encountered abuse, we were shocked and felt endangered and we didn't want to feel that again. We may have become worrywarts at a very early age, trying to prepare ourselves against being tripped up by more abuse.

Today I realize that worry does not offer any real protection. It only wears me down and makes me less capable when it comes time to deal with a crisis. If I am spending much of my time trying to predict the outcome of circumstances, or doing postmortems of past events, I will try turning my worry over to my higher power. I will do some deep breathing, exercise, or whatever works for me to reach a calmer state of mind.

I deserve peace and serenity. I do not need to be in a constant state of ready alert. I only need to be fully present.

I will keep myself in good condition with daily exercises for my physical, emotional, and spiritual well-being.

In my family of origin, I had little sense of balance. I lurched forward from crisis to crisis. It was often necessary for my survival to keep my true self in hiding, protected from those in authority who abused me. It was not possible to develop a center, a sense of well-being under these circumstances.

Today I am free to learn how to take good care of myself. I believe that exercise is a form of self-care. A regular schedule of exercise planned into my day—whether for my physical body, my spiritual practice, or my emotional development—can provide me with a structure for consistent self-care. Exercise will tone each of these systems so that I am in better shape when difficult situations arise. I will take pleasure both from the effects of the exercise and from the process. I will allow it to be an experience that brings me to the now, and I will do my best to participate with my full concentration. I will note that this time is well spent and rewards me with a sense of health.

*By making a written inventory of the times I
was sexually abused and the ways I was
affected, I see both the damages and the work
of my healing more clearly.*

A common problem for incest survivors is that
even after we have spoken out about the incidents we remember, we go on questioning ourselves. "Perhaps I made that up. . . ." "Perhaps it
wasn't all that bad. . . ." "I have taken a simple slip
of the hand and made it into a terrible thing. . . ."
"Even if I experienced those awful enemas as
rapes, I doubt that my parent had any idea what
he or she was doing. . . ." "Haven't I gotten all
out of whack and started exaggerating everything
that was done to me as a child?"

One way to counter some of my self-doubt and
stay away from minimizing and feeling discounted (because I have discounted myself) is to
make a written inventory of those times I remember in detail and document the effects of these experiences. I may want to go on and write an
account of how I've behaved sexually since the
incest. Did I become promiscuous? Did I become
withdrawn? Did I split off and treat sex as if it
were a sport? My inventory helps me both see
where I am now and where I am going.

I am never alone; my higher power becomes available to me as soon as I remember I have one.

For years some of us have lived without a sense of our spirituality, or with a sense that we had to reject and abandon our childhood spirituality as naive and inadequate because it had not spared us the abuse. Our life was devoid of any conscious connection with a higher power. We may have striven for greater and greater control, as if we, as drivers at the helm, were the highest power and were going to get things straightened out for ourselves.

I lived in spiritual bankruptcy for a long time, assuming it was possible for me to know best and be in charge. But this only allowed my obsessions and addictions to thrive, overpower me, and carry me to a bottom.

Today I open my heart to welcome a sense of my higher power. When I am deep in frustration, I do not need to grasp more tightly onto a problem but to turn it over to my higher power. Whether in joy or in sorrow, I do not need to feel alone. I can simply remember that my higher power is one with me and my decisions are being guided for my benefit long before I can see that benefit.

I choose to celebrate my holidays in the present, leaving the past in its place.

Family holidays can be very painful for those of us who have disturbing associations with past holidays. In my family of origin, Christmas was a day that exaggerated the discrepancy between the appearance of the family's "goodness" and the reality I experienced. Absorbing this dissonance was stressful and required an even greater stretch than usual of my ability to hold it all together.

Today I have the opportunity in recovery to make the holidays my own. I do not need to fake feelings or give gifts I do not feel inclined to give. I can tap the well of my newly developing spirituality, regardless of whatever religious training I received in the past. I can give myself the most important gift of respecting first my own needs and desires. When I have done this, I will find myself able to open up and share my love with others. I will feel fully a part of my own celebration and at one with the spirit of the universe.

I will erect my boundaries in a way that cares for my needs.

In the incest experience my boundaries were invaded, perhaps at a very young age, perhaps repeatedly. How then was I to know that I was entitled to have them respected?

In recovery I work diligently to become aware that I am in charge of creating and maintaining my boundaries. Whenever I feel as if I am being revictimized, I need to notice where I have left a door open that I needed to close. Have I returned to a pattern of taking care of someone else's needs while abandoning my own?

It does not come quickly or easily for me to respect my boundaries. When I realize I have neglected them or let other people, places, and things invade them, I seek the guidance I need to find my way back to my path. I do not need to castigate myself for not maintaining my boundaries perfectly. I concentrate once again on restoring them so that they become limits that support me.

In darkness or in joy, I am grateful to be able to experience and accept my feelings.

This date, the winter solstice, marks the shortest day of the year. It comes amidst the holiday season, when frenzy seems to be the order of the day. If I feel sad or bleak, I do not need to cover up those feelings or pretend to feel any other way. That only leads to having my true self buried and feeling revictimized. It is not surprising that the darkest time of the year may arouse dark feelings inside me.

The wonder is that even when I have these feelings, I have hope. I have vision that I am not alone or abandoned, and that I can find my way to the places where people will hear me speak my true feelings. For this I am grateful. I take a minute to think of all those out there still keeping the secret of incest.

Today I take the time to talk to my inner child—to communicate my love and acceptance to her and express my sorrow for the experiences she suffered. I assure her that I am working hard to protect her and am committed to staying with her, not rejecting her and abandoning her as others showed me how to do. I am grateful to her for having kept the secret when that was necessary.

I see the light within me; it illuminates my struggle with the darkness.

Many of us who have been abused are literally afraid of the dark, unable to sleep without a light on, fearful of entering a dark car or walking down a street at night. We've been primed in those fears by very real incidents that robbed us of our confidence. But our fears may also be compounded by the darkness we feel inside us—the despair and hopelessness we experienced in our victimization.

To heal I must enter my own darkness. It may feel excruciating to return to my past preserved in a dark well in my body. To go down deep as if into a dungeon, removing layers of protection that have shrouded me. To see there at the bottom of the well that I am not a bad seed. I am wounded, I am enraged, I am needy, and still I can love that naked person I am seeing. And with love I can birth that child into the light.

Just as the days grow longer after the solstice, the light in me will grow more radiant and illuminate a perspective that shows me where I've been and where I'm going.

I will ask for all the time and guidance I need before making a major decision.

As an incest survivor it has not been easy for me to act on my own behalf, to make choices that solely or primarily benefit me. I grew up feeling as if I had no choice but to go along with others. It was too painful to keep my own wants and needs in the forefront of my mind, so I hid them away in the corners. Many times I hid them so well I could not find them.

In recovery I must let them surface and be recognized. Then I am ready to act to satisfy them. I will have to choose between options that come my way; my road will fork and I will have to choose which way to go. When I become confused over my choices, it will help me to stop to talk with others—to air my feelings and allow my ambivalence to be expressed. Some of that ambivalence may come from the old voices inside me, provoked by my new attention to my best interests. Even after I have made a decision and taken action, these voices may continue to plague me with feelings of doubt and fear. But I will recognize them for what they are, admit that I was wounded and am still affected by the incest, and continue to go forth and blossom.

I create a family of my choice and take satisfaction from my bonding with them in love and generosity.

The neglect and abuse of my childhood will never be righted. It will come to rest in the place where it belongs—the past—but it cannot be changed. What I can do is create a safe and generous atmosphere in which my inner child as well as my adult self can relax and thrive. One way I can do this is to create and honor a family of my choice.

This can be a family of my friends alone, or a family of my chosen partner, our children, and our friends. I allow myself to love and be loved by this family. I learn that neglecting others will never correct the neglect I encountered, that generosity begets generosity.

On holidays or special days, I celebrate with this chosen family. When the old record plays, "This is not enough. You wanted this kind of real love from your biological family and that is the only place you can get what you really need," I will simply pick up the needle and place it in its cradle. I may be saddened by my losses, but I can turn toward, not away from, my chosen family in response.

I will be fully aware today and let Christmas be what I want it to be to express and celebrate my present.

For many of us Christmas hangs heavy with memories, moments of joy mixed up with grave disappointments. The dissonance between what we were supposed to feel and how we actually felt inside burdened us. Expectations in society at large for the closeness of family life exaggerated our predicament. And because it was a stressful time, we may have received more abuse than ever.

Today I need to decontaminate Christmas. I need to be able to celebrate it with the feeling that I am not separating from my pain or abandoning my true self. I take the day in the current year and remove all the overlay of years past, allowing it to become a holiday that celebrates my recovery. It is a holiday of the birth of light and spirit. I have a growing light within me. I am learning to give the gift of love and today is a good day to celebrate that by giving.

My recovery is an opportunity to fill with my spirit and become a beacon of healing to others.

Childhood sexual abuse creates dispirited children who learn to hide their deepest feelings and plug through life afraid to allow themselves lightness. We are familiar with, yet also afraid of the dark. Often, for protection, we develop a flat affect. Then, living this way, we identify ourselves with a picture of lifeless individuals—dull, boring, nondescript.

In recovery I realize this lifelessness was a defense, much like a possum playing dead. Day by day I emerge from it into a new light. I let my spirit glow and find expression. I do not need to be hidden. Sometimes it is frightening to be more fully known, yet I am no longer a child who is going to be abused again and there is no reason for me to live as though I am. I can honor my fear without letting it put me back there.

I let my light shine. It becomes a beacon to others with whom I share the gift of healing.

I encourage myself to grow and change despite fears aroused by the unfamiliar.

Even after I have become aware that it does not work in my favor, I often cling to an old way, believing there is comfort in its familiarity. Trying out new behavior and exploring new places in myself require risk, which is always accompanied by the tenderness of something newly born and not yet seasoned or experienced. I may be reluctant to feel the vulnerability of this state. I may cling tightly to the familiar as if it is the only way that can provide safety.

None of those old ways ever made me safe. Yet my impulses as I seek safety are rooted in that old naked sense of vulnerability.

I will recognize and care for my wounds and free myself to move through change. I will seek safety in a way that helps me do this with the awareness of my higher self.

*I let my inner child know it is safe now to play,
let myself become truly playful, and enjoy it.*

A child's spirit is naturally playful and finds the simplest things to play with. Witness a baby in a crib whose eyes play with light, whether from the sun or a light bulb. In an abusive family the child's playful spirit becomes hidden, a requirement for its survival.

In my healing I realize how greatly I've deprived myself by suppressing my playfulness. I feel as if I missed out on most of my childhood and carried my grim attitude into adult life. I sometimes approach everything with grave seriousness, perhaps giving small details more value than they deserve.

Today I can consciously call up my playful self and tell her I want to go out and romp. I want to run on the beach, play with words in a poem, whistle or sing, tap my partner on the shoulder and say, "Can we play together today?" Just for today I trust that the world will not fall apart because I choose to play. I will take in the results honestly and try playing more often.

I no longer bludgeon myself with criticism. I can even learn to benefit from it.

The fragility of my inner child made it very difficult for me to take criticism. I did not cause that fragility nor was I born with it. It resulted from the abuse experiences that fractured my psyche. Consequently, my response to criticism was to strive for perfection, to leave no openings for others to criticize me.

As I heal I realize that I do not need to hold onto my perfectionism. Even when I clutched to it, I still made mistakes. This is the nature of being human.

Criticism can be useful if I establish the inner strength to know when to trust and receive it. I do not need to be reluctant to assess the motives of the person who is criticizing me and take my assessment into account. When the critic is trustworthy, critical feedback can be an act of love that offers me perspective. It can help me broaden my viewpoint. It can let me see where my vision may have been clouded.

I will release feelings of negativity or self-loathing about my past ways of being.

Victimized by my incest experience, I have spent much of my life putting myself into situations where I became passive and felt revictimized. I have often felt subject to the whims of another. I have tolerated much abuse and hated myself for it. For if I were a lovable person, why would this be happening to me?

Today I realize that my psyche had no choice but to repeatedly return me to the trauma of the abuse until I could finally begin to see it and become willing to work with it. Having allowed abuse to be heaped on me in the past does not prove that I am a bad person. As I grow away from these behaviors and declare them unacceptable, I need not reject and shun my past self. Rather I need to embrace her, acknowledge her woundedness and all that she suffered.

When I see others behave in ways that bring on victimization, I can practice compassion for them rather than reject them out of contempt. This hand I reach out benefits them and helps me heal from the effects of self-hatred.

I allow myself conscious reflection at the end of the year, looking back over and realizing my progress in all areas of my life.

There is nothing wrong with looking back over the year as it ends, unless I use my reflection to beat up on myself and compare myself to perfectionistic goals. If I take stock as a company would inventory a supply room, I will become better known to myself and likely end up composing a gratitude list. For I will become aware of what I *have* rather than what I *don't have*.

As I look back I note the great strides I have made in my recovery. These may include facing memories, confronting someone when I needed to stand up for myself, speaking out without shame about incest, walking away from abusive situations, nurturing and protecting my inner child, grieving for my stolen childhood, recognizing my rage and using appropriate outlets for it, and building trust in my higher power.

I reflect on other areas of my life as well. Have I taken better care of my health? Have I allowed myself to give and receive love? Have I entered life more fully? When I look at life this way I see my cup is more than half full. There is no emptiness unless I choose to approach myself from a negative direction.

INDEX

Owning Ourselves—Sept. 5